Glimpses of Chiswick's Development

The Author in his office
1962

Glimpses of Chiswick's Development

WILLIAM P. ROE
F.R.I.C.S.

To Francesca
With very best wishes
William P. Roe

1999

Published by William P. Roe
14 Alwyn Avenue, Chiswick London W4 4PB

ISBN 0 9516512 2 6

Design and typesetting by
John Saunders Design and Production, Reading
Printed and bound in Great Britain by
Biddles Ltd., Guildford and King's Lynn

Contents

Illustrations

Introduction

READERS of my earlier books "Glimpses of Chiswick's Place in History" and "Glimpses of World War II" printed in 1990 and 1991 respectively, will be aware that I was born in Chiswick, was educated in Chiswick, and worked in Chiswick (apart from some six and half years military service during the Second World War) with the same firm of Messrs. Tyser, Greenwood & Company, until I, and my partner in that firm, George Bradley, retired in 1985.

As both my partner and myself had been given the opportunity of becoming partners in that firm of Surveyors, Valuers & Auctioneers when we duly qualified in the profession, so we wished to accept into partnership young men in our employment who were suitably qualified and able to continue the business after we had retired.

For that reason I imagined that, in the event of need, I would be able to have access to the considerable records that had been stored away in the offices at 386 Chiswick High Road. In the event, however, that proved to be short lived, because practices such as Messrs. Tyser, Greenwood & Company were the subject of acquisition by Building Societies and Insurance Companies who wished to form large groups of offices, particularly estate agency offices, which they would control and, hopefully, reap the financial benefits which increased annually during the latter part of the 1980's.

As a result of such an acquisition of Messrs. Tyser, Greenwood & Company, followed by a resale, and yet another resale, much of those records virtually disappeared and one document, in particular, that disappeared was one of two copies of an auction particular giving details of an auction sale held by the original Richard Tyser, over a hundred years ago.

During the course of writing this book, I became conscious that inevitably I would overlook many of the changes and redevelopments that took place in Chiswick, the date and detail of which I am not able to recall with any accuracy. I am aware, for instance, that I have omitted to make any reference to the closing of the old Gunnersbury Congregational Church, off the south side of the High Road between King's Place and Marlborough Road, which was demolished and the site redeveloped commercially, whilst on the other side of the High Road, on the corner of Chiswick Road, Alfred Herbert, the machine tool company, acquired a number of premises to redevelop as their own workshop. They were required by the local planning authority to provide a number of residential units in place of those demolished by the scheme, so they built a tower with a residential unit on each floor.

Then there must have been a number of small developments that took place some years ago which I have failed to recall, including a number of the larger houses in the Gunnersbury area, many in the Chiswick High Road, which were demolished and redeveloped as small blocks of modern flats, one being named "Tomlinson House" to acknowledge the original developer in that area William John Tomlinson. Similarly, a number of the larger houses in Wellesley Road have either been converted into flats or demolished from time to time and modern dwellings erected on the sites.

Barrowgate Road, which in Victorian times had large houses principally only on the northern side overlooking open fields to the south, with the occasional large building on the other side on the corner of Park Road (opposite to the original houses in Dukes Avenue), also "Garthowen" at number seventy-eight, between which two houses, during the late 1920's and the early 1930's a number of two story houses had been built. Some of the larger houses on the northern side have again either been converted into flats or the houses demolished and the site redeveloped, also sites between those houses developed with modern dwellings. One site in that road was acquired during the post second world war period by a Chiswick builder, Richard Ball, who built thereon his own fine detached house. He also built other new residential buildings in the Chiswick area including a short row of "town houses" in Chatsworth Road; a small block of flats on the east side of Park Road just south of the entrance into Chiswick House Grounds, and another small block of flats on the corner of Bolton Road and Cavendish Road. Richard Ball also acquired a site on the west side of Garth Road, a short cul-de-sac which runs south beside Garthowen, and built a short terrace of four houses with unusual internal design. In addition, he built a detached, two floored house beside number two Devonshire Gardens, and having acquired Jackson's builders premises on the corner of Burlington Lane and Wilmington Avenue, he erected on the cleared site, another fine two-floored house.

CHAPTER ONE

"The Victorian Era"

A BOOK written by Mr. and Mrs. S.C. Hall and published in 1859, entitled "The Book of the Thames" contains the following comment:

> There are few localities in the vicinity of London so interesting as the pleasant village of Chiswick.

It is possible that Mr. and Mrs Hall were referring to the riverside area just west of Hammersmith, known as Old Chiswick, with its parish church of St. Nicholas. The bulk of the area now known as Chiswick is contained on three sides by the River Thames, and in those days the majority of the land within that area was predominately occupied as market gardens, meadowland and orchards, although some land had already begun to be taken over for both business purposes and for housing of the ever increasing population.

Chiswick as we know it today comprises not only the manor of Old Chiswick, but also the manor of Little Sutton; the other riverside area just east of Brentford known as Strand-on-the-Green, and the considerable area in the centre known as Turnham Green which, in the mid-nineteenth century, was a much larger area than remains today. In addition, Turnham Green was provided with its own parish church built within the commonland of Turnham

Green in 1843, but still remained under the administration of the manor of Old Chiswick until 1870.

In that year of 1870, a home for motherless children was built on a corner site close to Grove Park House, in the southern part of Chiswick, east of Strand-on-the-Green and the home was named "The Roystons".Records illustrate that the population of all areas of Chiswick almost doubled between 1871 and 1881.

It was in 1873 that Mr. Richard Tyser opened his small estate agency and auctioneering business in offices at number 360 High Road, in the Turnham Green area. In all probability, Richard Tyser was not a Chiswick man but someone drawn to Chiswick by the prospects of a reasonably good living in land and property dealing.

In an endeavour to visualise what the area of Turnham Green was like in 1873, one is assisted by the oldest known photograph of the area which is reproduced in Carolyn and Peter Hammond's book entitled "The Old Photographs Series – Chiswick" which shows a panorama of the High Road, on the evening of 16th August 1863, taken from the Green looking North, with the "Crown and Anchor" public house in a central position and the Wellington Terrace of houses to the east (unfortunately not extending to Richard Tyser's offices at number 360 High Road), and various properties to the west, including a single-floored smithy and Essex Place, with what appears to be open countryside behind those buildings. It is possible that one of those buildings was a Friends Meeting House that existed in Essex Place until 1920.

In that picture there is a pump on the edge of Turnham Green, with newly planted young trees along the boundary with the High Road, the boundary being marked by fencing of posts and single rail. Also shown within the photograph, is part of the pond which then existed on the eastern corner of the Green.

The High Road, which was still being referred to as the "Brentford Road" as it led from London across Turnham Green to Brentford, still contained a number of large houses, many built during the eighteenth century and some even earlier, also quite a number of inns and public houses, such as the "Robin Hood" on the corner of Acton Green Road (later named Acton Lane), with the old inn known as "The Packhorse" on the eastern corner of that turning.

West of Wellington Terrace was "Belmont House", then "Holly House" (both giving their names to roads constructed at those places), with Fisher's Lane further east, then a terrace of properties known as "Queen's Row" stretching up to Bond Street, on the other side of which was "Albert Place" extending up to "The Windmill", a public house which had occupied that site since 1717, and which was rebuilt at the end of the nineteenth century by the brewers, Fuller, Smith and Turner, from the Old Chiswick area.

On the west side of Turnham Green, in Sutton Lane, and facing the Green, there existed the large residence known as "The Chestnuts", also Arlington Park House. On the south side of the High Road, set well back by paddocks from the alternatively dusty and muddy carriageway of the main road, was the public house named "The Barley Mow"; then "Bleak House" and King's Row between them and the Duke of Devonshire's private avenue of lime trees which extended southward from the High Road into the grounds of his Chiswick House, with the Lodge situated on the eastern side of the avenue, well back from the main road.

To the east of the Lodge was "Afton House"; "Bolton House"; "Linden House"; "Campden House" and the public house named "George IV" before Chiswick Field Lane (later renamed "Devonshire Road"), with "Sulhamstead House" and "Annandale House" on the eastern side of Chiswick Field Lane, also another inn known as "The Packhorse and Talbot".

Before the middle of the nineteenth century, a number of workmen's dwellings were built on a site on the north side of Hogarth Lane and west of the bottom end of Chiswick Field

Lane, and that development was named "Chiswick New Town", to which was added, in 1848, a church called the Chapel of Saint Mary Magdalene. Those workmen's houses were of poor quality intended for the families of the people working in the nearby market gardens; orchards; breweries and other industries, so they were of mean measurement with their front doors opening directly onto the roads which were not properly paved until the 1880's by which time other developments had taken place nearby.

Most of those early developments, certainly the "New Chiswick" houses, were demolished in the early 1950's, shortly after the end of the Second World War. There existed a "British National School Room" next to cottages in Fishermans Place (earlier known as "Slut's Hole"), close to St. Nicholas Church, the parish church of Old Chiswick, and that school was supplemented in the middle of the nineteenth century, by further British National School Rooms at Turnham Green, that for the boys in Essex Place Square, and for Infants and Girls in Horticultural Place on the south side of the Green.

In 1849 the London and South Western Railway Company was constructing one of their railway lines which cut across parts of Chiswick, notably through some late Georgian houses in Grove Park Terrace, which crossing was left without a formal controlled crossing until 1868, when a footbridge was also constructed over the railway.

The construction of railway lines at that time also resulted in the northern section of the "Back Common" part of Turnham Green, being severed from the rest, due to the need to construct an embankment so that the railway line could pass over Turnham Green Terrace.

Never-the-less, the introduction of the railways added to the desirability of the Chiswick Area for residential and commercial development.

In 1869, two railway stations were opened, the first in

Turnham Green Terrace and named "Turnham Green", and the other at the western end of Chiswick which was named "Brentford Road Station" (after the original name of Chiswick High Road) but that was changed to "Gunnersbury Station" in 1871, and a further line was added, in 1879, from Turnham Green Station to Ealing. When the London and South Western Railway Company extended their railway line to Richmond in 1897/8, it was necessary for them to build a bridge across the River Thames, between the two old inns on Strand-on-the-Green, the "Bull" and the "City Barge". At that same time the Company also closed a level crossing at the bottom of Sutton Court Road and replaced it with the Grove Park road bridge.

At the Kew Bridge end of Strand-on-the-Green a French Steam Laundry had become established in 1860 and remained until 1905 when it moved to the other side of the Back Lane (later Thames Road) and became known as the Pier House Laundry.

As early as 1858 a haberdashery and household goods store was opened in the High Road, close to the "Windmill" public house, in the name of "Rankins" and it remained open until the mid-1950's when the store was taken over by Salems for the sale of carpets. The premises were demolished and redeveloped some fifteen years later, and part of the premises became occupied by Dillons, the booksellers.

Heathfield House, the home of the first Baron Heathfield, who was formerly known as General George Elliott of Gibralter fame, existed on the south side of Turnham Green until 1865, when it was demolished and Heathfield Gardens was developed, followed in 1867 by the erection on the corner of Heathfield Gardens and Sutton Lane, of the Christ Church Vicarage.

Chiswick only narrowly avoided becoming part of the London County Council in 1868, but remained within the administrative County of Middlesex until 1965 when it became the eastern tip of the Greater London Borough of Hounslow.

During 1864 John I. Thornycroft, a steam yacht and launch builder, established his works at Church Wharf on the river front, close to St. Nicholas Church, and he was later joined by his brother-in-law, John Donaldson. Together they established a flourishing business by pioneering the screw propelled naval craft which became too large by 1904, so they removed to their new works at Southampton. John I. Thornycroft had already provided a steam driven, double decker omnibus which was used to provide public transport between Oxford Circus and Hammersmith. The son of John I. Thornycroft built a large house in Chiswick Lane, in 1875, known as "The Tower House" which later became the home of the Missionary" Sisters of Verona".

Another family of manufacturers, by the name of Mason, established the Chiswick Soap and Polish Company in 1870, which later adopted the name of "The Cherry Blossom Polish Company" and, some years later, changed its name again to "Chiswick Products" before amalgamating, in 1954, with the firm of Reckitt and Colman.

Some land along the southern boundary of the Royal Horticultural Society's grounds was released for house development during 1870, and some large houses were built fronting Barrowgate Road.

Not long after the construction of the railway across Grove Park Terrace by London and South Western Railway Company in the mid-nineteenth century, some large houses of gothic style were built beside Maynards Boat House, at the eastern end of Strand-on-the-Green, facing Grove Park Road, also a firm of builders, Messrs. R. Arundell and Son, erected "Clifton Works" beside the railway line in Grove Park Terrace, and they commenced building a number of houses alongside their works, also along Grove Park Road and Gardens, which when occupied led to the formation in the 1870's of the "Grove Park Society". Also, during 1872, a third Anglican Parish Church was built in the

Chiswick area, with funds generously donated by His Grace, the Duke of Devonshire, on a site at the junction of Hartington Road and Grove Park Road, named "St. Pauls Church".

The Southern Railway Chiswick Station was originally intended to provide access to the sporting facilities in that area, such as the University and Polytechnic boat houses and sports grounds, and one of the earliest buildings erected near to the railway station, was the Grove Park Hotel, but soon other residential building took place including "Holly Lodge" in Bolton Road and "Ranelagh House", "Hughenden House" and the old "Lindens" in Hartington Road, the latter subsequently demolished and redeveloped. In 1898, a large, detached house was built in Grove Park Gardens for the Bellamy family, named "Belfairs", which subsequently became a Council Home for the elderly. In addition to those house developments, William J. Tomlinson commenced building houses in another part of Chiswick, well to the West of Turnham Green, thereby creating Oxford and Cambridge Roads (in honour of the University boat race), also Harvard Road, named after the American university whose team rowed against the other two teams at that time. He extended his house building to the northern side of the High Road, and created Silver Crescent and Thorney Hedge Road in the process.

The Army and Navy Depository was built in 1871, close to the militia barracks in Barley Mow Passage, at the Prospect Place corner with Heathfield Terrace. In 1874, not long after Richard Tyser had set up his offices in Chiswick High Road, a piece of land on the south side of Turnham Green and just north of the Royal Horticultural Society's grounds and facing Heathfield Terrace, was acquired and conveyed to the Churchwardens and Overseers, so that a Vestry Hall could be erected thereon for their own use. Also in 1874, William Trehearne, the surveyor to the Chiswick Improvement Commissioners, built a large house for his own occupation, close to the Brentford Road Railway Station (later renamed "Gunnersbury") and the house was later occupied by Alfred Kendall who developed Grange Road in the 1890's. That large house, which had been named "The Grange", was demolished in the 1930's and the block of flats built on its site retained that name.

Yet another development that occurred in 1874 was the erection of the Chiswick Police Station on the eastern corner of the High Road with Windmill Road. During 1875, Jonathan T. Carr planned a new concept in urban housing and created a "Garden Suburb" to the north of Turnham Green Station, which concept involved having an Act of Parliament passed whereby, in 1879, a portion of land within the Parish of Ealing was transferred to the Parish of Chiswick. The history of that remarkable development is contained in a book by the late T. Affleck Greeves.

To provide dwellings for the workers required by the expanding manufacturing businesses, further residential development took place, including the development of an area west of Chiswick Field Lane (Devonshire Road) and north of the New Chiswick Estate. That estate of artisan dwellings became known as the "Glebe Estate" as it was commenced on ecclesiastical land east of Dukes Avenue and south of Bourne Place, the road linking Chiswick Field Lane and the southern end of Bolton Gardens, being named "Glebe Street", from which another road ran south, parallel to Chiswick Field Lane, to Devonshire Place, and that road was named Dale Street. Bolton Gardens was extended southward, parallel to Dale Street, and was named Duke Road, and the roads between those two roads were named Binns Road; Reckitt Road; Quick Road and Fraser Street, suggesting that they were probably the names of the various tradesmen employed in carrying out the development. The name of Duke Road was later applied to that first section of road out of the High Road which had been originally named Bolton Gardens.

Chiswick Mall, which contained a number a fine dwellings built during the seventeenth and eighteenth centuries, were subject, in

1875, to various changes, including the demolition of "College House" and Suffolk House", and the building of three houses on the site named "Heron House"; "Thames Bank" and "Staithe House".

In 1876, opposite to the gothic houses in Grove Park Road, a large house was built and named "Isis House" which was converted, some fifty years later, into a number of flats and renamed "Isis Court".

The Improvements Board (which later became the Chiswick Local Board), arranged during 1878, for the provision of sewage works close to the river, off Corney Road. The large houses along Chiswick High Road, some of which were erected during the eighteenth century, began to be demolished and the sites redeveloped. In 1878 "Linden House" with extensive grounds enabled Linden Gardens to be built, and in 1880 another named "Annandale House" (the home of the Marquess of Annandale) and the adjoining house, "Sulhamstead House", were demolished and Annandale Road created, almost immediately opposite to Turnham Green Terrace. On the north side of the High Road, "Myrtle Cottage", just west of Fishers Lane, was demolished and on its site a row of shops were erected and occupied the space up to Holly Road.

"Stile Hall", a large residence, built in the latter quarter of the eighteenth century, close to the corner of Wellesley Road (named after the family name of the Duke of Wellington) and Chiswick High Road where it joins Kew Bridge Road, came into the ownership of the Right Honorable R.R. Bignell.

Another development in 1880, away from the High Road, was on a site on the west side of Sutton Court Road and the south side of Barrowgate Road. That site had been acquired on generous terms from His Grace the Duke of Devonshire, by the Wesleyan Methodist Church whose members built, in the centre of the site facing Sutton Court Road, a large Sunday School which was also used for Sunday Worship and a number of weekday activities. A house for a resident Minister was erected just south of the Hall, in 1902, and that was followed, in 1909, by the erection of a large church on the corner of Barrowgate Road with Sutton Court Road. Also in 1880, Mr. R.T. Smith, an employee of Thornycrofts, founded the Chiswick Mission Hall in Fraser Street, close to the corner of Dale Street.

Another non-conformist group of Christians, who were known as the Primitive Methodists, having established their meeting in a rented room in Devonshire Road, found themselves able to use an old Chiswick Lane chapel, but in 1881 they acquired a site on the east side of Fishers Lane, on which they erected a Mission Church and School premises. Those premises were destroyed by enemy bombing during the Second World War. In 1882, work commenced on the building of another Anglican Church close to the junction of Sutton Lane with Fauconberg Road, and that became known as St. Michaels, Sutton Court. Four years later, the Roman Catholic "St. Mary's Church" was replaced by the red brick church on the corner of Dukes Avenue with the High Road, and was named "Our Lady of Grace". Also in 1886, some houses were built on the eastern side of Dukes Avenue, opposite to its junction with Barrowgate Road. That followed Dukes Avenue being taken over as a public road, it having remained a private road until 1880.

Another form of development took place, this time in the Bedford Park area, where the Polytechnic School in Bath Road was opened in October 1881. From 1882, horse drawn trams were introduced to Chiswick High Road, the horses being stabled in Stamford Brook Road until 1909. However, the tram lines were adapted for the electric trams which were introduced in 1901, following the building of Power House, adjoining the Tram Depot on the north side of the eastern end of the High Road.

It is recorded that the painter, Vincent Van Gogh, as an apprentice preacher, was staying with Rev. Thomas Jones, the principal of a Methodist school in Twickenham Road, Isleworth, in 1876, and he journeyed to a small chapel at Turnham Green, which is believed to be on a site west of Sutton Lane just north of Chiswick High Road, and in 1882 a large stone church was built for the Congregational denomination, adjacent to that chapel. Another school was built and opened in 1884, on the north side of Hogarth Lane at the southern end of Duke Road, and inevitably named "Hogarth School". A few years later, in 1886, another church was built in Wellesley Road for the Baptist community and became known as the Gunnersbury Baptist Church, and that was followed a year later by another Anglican Church which was built of Norfolk stone on a site north of the High Road, between Thorney Hedge Road and Gunnersbury Lane, and that church was named "St. James Church", now no longer existing.

In the Little Sutton area, the Dancer family let their premises on the inner bend of Sutton Lane, to a relative by marriage, Benjamine F. Tappenden, as a dairy, which business was eventually sold in 1921, to the United Dairies. Further shop development occurred in the Turnham Green area of the High Road during 1887, when the Crown & Anchor public house was altered and extended, and shops were built to the east of the new public house premises. The undertakers by the name of Barratts became established in that year of 1887 on the north side of the High Road, facing Turnham Green, close to the Old Pack Horse inn on the corner of Acton Green Road.

1890 introduced a number of new facilities for the Chiswick people, such as the opening of its first Public Library in Bourne Place, where it stayed for just eight years before being transferred to the family home of the Sandersons in Dukes Avenue, close to Barley Mow Passage. The Royal Mail opened the Chiswick Postal Sorting Office on the corner of Back Common Road and Clifton Gardens and it remained there until 1967. Its position there explains why so much of the southern parts of Acton shares the postal code of "W4" with the whole of Chiswick. Those and other advancements towards urbanising and modernising Chiswick should be viewed, never-the-less, with the fact that up until 1890, eel boats were common on the river at Chiswick.

It was probably about 1885 that Richard Tyser employed a young lad by the name of Ernest Parsons for general office duties which included collecting the rents of properties owned by various landlords for whom Richard Tyser was their agent. Ernest Parsons didn't realise at that time that he was destined to serve not only Richard Tyser, but the Company thereafter for nearly sixty-five years before he died. Unfortunately there has been very little information disclosed about Richard Tyser, but Ernest Parsons used to recall that his duties included meeting Richard Tyser each morning when he arrived in his pony and trap, then stabling the pony and garaging the trap, and reversing the procedure each evening; also virtually every day, one of his tasks was to purchase a lamb chop and cook it over the open fire in the office at 360 Chiswick High Road for Richard Tyser's lunch.

Richard Tyser is understood to have held his public auctions of properties in a well known local tavern and he ensured that a period of up to one hour, prior to the commencement of the auction sale, was available so that prospective purchasers could rest from their travelling to the auction, also thereby affording time for them to have partaken of sufficient good cheer to loosen their tongues for brisk bidding at the actual auction sale.

At this point, perhaps it might be advisable to remind readers that the acquisition and ownership of properties, in those days, was mainly confined to the people of some personal wealth, also nearly all forms of newly developed property were destined to be leased, or rented, to tenants. In the case of the poorer class of residential properties, it could prove extremely difficult to catch the tenant (almost always the husband and father of the occupying family), before he had spent all of his wages, and Ernest Parsons, whose jobs included collecting those rents for Mr. Tyser, explained that the busiest time for him was on Friday night each week, seeking out the various tenants, sometimes at home, but often either at one of the local markets, or in a local public house, in order to extract the weekly rent from them before all their cash was spent.

In 1891 there were seven butcher's slaughter-houses in Chiswick, one of the oldest of which was "Caughts" situated on the north side of the High Road between Essex Place Square and Acton Lane, facing Turnham Green, established in 1852, but closed in 1959. It is reported that if a cricket batsman playing on Turnham Green, managed to hit the ball from the Green, over the High Road, into Caught's forecourt, he would be awarded a leg of lamb.

Stile Hall House was demolished in 1891 and the houses in Stilehall Gardens were built on the site; also the first Chiswick Fire Station was built in that year, complete with a tower, on the south side of the High Road, next to Gerrards hardware store, between Linden Gardens and Devonshire Road. Two years later, more shops were built on the north side of the High Road, opposite to Chiswick Lane, when the Roebuck Inn, a single storey major coaching inn, licenced from 1761, and its adjoining stables, were demolished and the Roebuck rebuilt. At about the same time, Thornton Avenue was developed, turning north out of the High Road and bending at right angles to join Turnhams Green Terrace, close to the railway station.

William Soper opened a store in 1893, on the north side of the High Road, just east of Turnham Green, occupying four shops, which store was acquired in 1919 by Percy Goodban, thereby changing its name, and it remained an attractive shopping venue until it eventually closed in 1974. Bissley's printing works were established in 1894, on a site between Caughts, the butcher, and the Old Packhorse Inn, but the site became part of Oswald Stoll's Chiswick Empire development, some years later.

That year of 1894, saw the setting up of the Urban District Council of Chiswick, in place of the Chiswick Local Board; also, at the Hammersmith end of the High Road, Young's Corner premises were rebuilt as a part of a redevelopment scheme. A local weekly newspaper entitles "The Chiswick Times" was first published on 29th March 1895, by which time Mr. Richard Tyser had opened another office at Gunnersbury Railway Station, and had a Mr. Chamberlain as a partner. The firm under the name of Messrs. Tyser & Chamberlain, Auctioneers, Practical Surveyors and Valuers, Land, House and Estate Agents, arranged with the publishers of the Chiswick Times to have a space reserved for the firm's various announcements, including public auctions, on the top left corner of the Public Announcements page, and that space was retained for over eighty years. However, almost immediately thereafter, Mr. Chamberlain's name disappeared and Mr. Ernest Greenwood, a comparatively young man, became partner to Richard Tyser, and the firm became known as Messrs Tyser Greenwood. A small book entitled "The Law of Landlord & Tenant" by Mr. A. Hodsworth, contains Ernest Greenwood's signature and the date "1896".

When the London and South-Western Railway Company extended their railway lines across the River Thames during the nineteenth century, their works cut across an old, long established lane, that ran from the water pump on Turnham Green southwards to Strand-on-the-Green, which lane had become known as "Dead Donkey Lane". The Magnolia Wharf works on the waterfront at Strand-on-the-Green, were extended to the north side of "Back Lane" (Thames Road), to the east of the railway line, and more workmen's houses were erected in Magnolia Road, also Herbert and Ernest Gardens, with a footbridge over the railway, and beside the railway line, the West London Timber Company established their works. The northern section of Dead Donkey Lane remained and the section from the footbridge became known as "Dean's Lane" with Mr. Shepherd's nursery gardens between the Lane and the railway line from Gunnersbury Station to Kew Gardens Railway Station.

Some better class residential development had also taken place at the northern end of Deans Lane, across the foot of Harvard Hill, in a road which was named Wolseley Gardens, and in roads which ran between it and Grove Park Terrace. One was named St. Mary's Grove which contained a variety of houses of different styles, some in two storey terraces; some semi-detached; some detatched; some with three storeys, and some double-fronted. The other road was named Burnaby Gardens, out of which (some years later) another road branched into Grove Park Terrace, named Burnaby Crescent. Across both those roads, from Sutton Lane to the end of Deans Lane, another residential road was constructed and named Gordon Road. General Gordon of Khartoum, and his colleague, Col. Frederick Burnaby, were undoubtedly the inspiration for the naming of those roads.

A pocket of orchard land had been left undeveloped north of Gordon Road and south of Wolseley Gardens, between the railway line and the backs of the houses in the shorter section of St. Mary's Grove, but in the last years of the nineteenth century, a Mr. John Norris commenced building houses on that orchard land, extending both Gordon Road and Wolseley Gardens westward, also constructing two roads between them which he named Whitehall Gardens and Whitehall Park Road, completing the development by 1900.

Lady Charlotte Boyle, the heiress of Richard Boyle, the third Earl of Burlington and the fourth Earl of Cork, married the Marquis of Hartington, the heir to His Grace the Duke Of Devonshire, which marriage resulted in the Burlington properties, such as Chiswick House, becoming part of the Duke's Cavendish

Estate. Subsequent Dukes made further acquisitions so that a great deal of the freehold land in the Chiswick area came within the same ownership, and accounts for the preponderance of "Devonshire" street names.

In 1896, three acres of land was acquired from the Duke Of Devonshire fronting Burlington Lane (named after the Earl of Burlington), on the corner of Corney Road, by the Sisterhood known as the Society of St. Margaret, who wished to set up an annex to St. Mary's Convent in Kensington, to be used as a hospital for poor, handicapped and incurable girls and women. Originally the Home was known as "St. Joseph's" with an operating theatre eventually being opened in 1912, but closed upon the outbreak of the second world war in 1939. Subsequently, the Home became known by the present title of "St. Mary's Convent and Nursing Home".

Demolitions and redevelopments continued in 1896, including the original "Robin Hood & Little John" beerhouse, which was just west of Acton Lane on the north side of the High Road, also two large houses in Chiswick Lane, one known as "Bradmore House" (on the east side at the southern end, built in the early part of the eighteenth century), and the other "Manor Farm House" which had been built at the end of the seventeenth century for the parliamentarian, Sir Stephen Fox, that house having been acquired by the Tuke family, towards the end of the eighteenth century, and used as a private lunatic asylum.

Following the demolition of Manor Farm House, the site was used for another estate of artisans dwellings, the roads being named alphabetically – Ashbourne; Balfern; Cornwall; Dorchester and Eastbury Groves.

A Grocery business, by the name of "Gapps Ltd." built their new store, in 1879, on the western corner of Acton Lane, on the north side of Chiswick High Road; and in that same year, a church was built on the east side of Annandale Road and became known as the Chiswick Baptist Church. Chiswick Public Library moved, in 1898, from Bourne Place into the large family house in Dukes Avenue, which had been generously donated by the Sanderson family. The Old Chiswick Parish of St. Nicholas opened their Church Hall, in 1889, at the southern end of Devonshire Road, on the corner of Mawson Lane.

In the meantime, auction sales were continuing to be held by Ernest Greenwood, who had taken control of Richard Tyser's business, and now traded under the name of "Tyser Greenwood", although by 1899 the size of the name "Tyser" had been reduced and the name of "Greenwood" enlarged. Also advertised was the fact that the firm's telephone number was "12 Hammersmith".

One such auction was advertised to take place at 2 o'clock on Tuesday, 1st August 1899, in the City of London, at "The Mart" in Tokenhouse Yard. That information is contained on a poster which has survived all those years, and offers for sale the remains of an estate comprising "23 Sound and Substantial Leasehold cottages known as 1 to 16 and 23 to 29 Dalton Road, the first turning on the right in Devonshire Road, Chiswick – in perfect repair, each let to excellent tenants at thirteen shillings per week". "Each house is built and arranged for two families".

The leasehold term still had sixty-six years unexpired, with an annual Ground Rent of four pound and ten shillings each house, suggesting that they were probably built in about 1866. Dalton Road subsequently became known as Prince of Wales Terrace.

Although there were some exceptions, the general practice in those days of development and redevelopment, was for the landlord (who was frequently either the Lord of the Manor, or a titled person with wealth – hence the name "landlord"), to grant building leases to an approved developer, the leases invariably being for the duration of ninety-nine years, at fairly nominal annual ground rents, although sometimes an individual ground rent was imposed on each of the properties to be erected on the site. Frequently those leases imposed restrictions as to the type and class of development to take place, and contained covenants in order to ensure subsequent proper maintenance of the properties. In effect, the leases were an early form of "Town Planning".

The better off tradesmen and professional gentlemen of that period often decided to purchase a group of such properties as those being offered by Messrs. Tyser Greenwood at their auction on 1st. August 1899, so as to leave them to their wives as a form of income should they become widowed.

Whereas there is no known evidence of professional attainment by Richard Tyser, there is evidence that Ernest Greenwood became a Practising Associate of the Surveyors Institution. The business of an Auctioneer and Estate Agent in the Victorian era was somewhat different from the rather more restricted practices of today. In those days it was quite acceptable for an agent to decide to purchase for himself a particular property he was asked to sell, and many such purchases were certainly made by the young Ernest Greenwood, presumably with the objective of providing an income upon his retirement, also to make available an income for his widow and family. Not long after the commencement of the twentieth century, however, such practices came into disfavour and the professional institutions condemned them.

At the Stamford Brook end of Chiswick High Road, where much of the land was still owned by the Ecclesiastical Commissioners, the aptly named Prebend Gardens was constructed between the north side of the High Road and Stamford Brook Green; also a large block of mansion flats was built on the south side of the High Road between Netheravon Road and Airedale Avenue, and that block was named Prebend Mansions. Turnham Green Terrace contained some handsome houses built in about 1800, on the east side of the road, and shops began to become established in the road during subsequent years, so the provision merchants, Durban & Allwrights, established their store a little further north on the eastern side of the Terrace, in 1900.

"Bohemia House" and two cottages on the northern side of the High Road, to the east of Turnham Green Terrace, were demolished, and a road developed named Bohemia Avenue, but the name subsequently became Ennismore Avenue.

The long Victorian era came to an end in 1901 and we entered the Edwardian era, which proved to be quite short.

CHAPTER TWO

"The Edwardian Era"

AN event that took place on 10th July 1901 heralded the very considerable advancement of mankinds achievements during the twentieth century. That event was the inauguration of the London United Electric Tramways at their headquarters in the tram depot on the north side of Chiswick High Road, beside which they built their "Power House". From there they operated tram services between Shepherds Bush and Uxbridge, also between Hounslow and Hampton Court and London.

Shortly before then, in February 1901, the new Chiswick Town Hall was opened following the extensive extension and rebuilding of the Vestry Hall situated on the corner of Heathfield Terrace and Sutton Court Road. The new premises, which were occupied by the Chiswick Urban District Council, included the Council Chamber, also the Devonshire Room and Hogarth Hall.

Thomas Nichols, a builder who then lived at "Vine House" in Church Street, commenced building houses, during 1902, in Airedale Avenue, a turning on the south side of the High Road, east of Chiswick Lane, down to Beverley Road, which itself formed the northern boundary to Homefields Recreation Grounds.

It is believed that Chiswick acquired its own telephone exchange in about 1903, when it occupied a large building in

Sutton Court Road, behind the Town Hall, at the north-west corner of the Royal Horticultural Grounds, and a "Chiswick" telephone number was acquired by Messrs. Tyser, Greenwood & Crier, which initially was "339".

In January 1902 one of the large houses which had been built in the Victorian Era in a road which ran south from Grove Park Road, close to the Chiswick Southern Railway Station, named Bolton Road, was occupied by Rev. Henry Montgomery, the Bishop of Tasmania. That was number nineteen and his two sons attended St. Paul's School, just across the border in Hammersmith, and one of those two sons was named Bernard Law Montgomery, then just fourteen years of age, but who became an army officer, saved from death by his batman during the First World War, and during the Second World War became possibly the best known army general renowned for his resounding victories at El Alamein, North Africa, Sicily, Italy, Normandy, Netherlands and Germany. A statue of Field Marshall Sir Bernard L. Montgomery, G.C.B., D.S.O. can be found outside the Ministry of Defence Building in Whitehall.

Between 1902 and 1904, C.F.A. Voysey designed and built for Mr. Sanderson, a rather unique factory building, faced externally with white glazed tiles, on the northern side of Barley Mow Passage, behind the shops in the High Road. By that time the High Road had become an established major shopping centre and in 1903, Boots the Chemist had opened two shops in Chiswick High Road.

The Royal Horticultural Society having acquired their new grounds at Wisley, commenced removing their Chiswick Grounds so that eventually only the name "Horticultural Place" remained beside the old National School on the south side of Turnham Green.

Around that time, Ernest Greenwood decided to abandon the small branch office at Gunnersbury Railway Station and had taken occupation of the Bedford Park Estate Office which was adjacent to the main entrance to Turnham Green "Underground" Railway Station close to the junction of Bath Road with Turnham Green Terrace. In addition, he opened another branch office at Barnes, in the Lowther Parade of shops and Mansion flats at the bend of Church Road into Castlenau, and that office used the telephone number from the Hammersmith exchange, whilst the Bedford Park Office had the telephone number of "Chiswick 135".

Ernest Greenwood's partner, at that time was a Mr. Crier, one of two brothers, the other brother being a District Surveyor in the Hammersmith area, and the title of the firm was "Messrs. Tyser, Greenwood & Crier". Under that name they arranged an auction to take place at two o'clock precisely, on 3rd June 1904, at the Mart, Token-house Yard, in the City of London. The property being offered on that occasion was described as "Valuable Freehold Building Plots, also two old fashion residences with large gardens, having a total frontage to Grove Park Road, Chiswick, of 180 feet, and a return frontage of 138 feet to Riverview Road and Back Lane (Thames Road), which was ripe for immediate development". The poster advertising the auction went on to state – "Possession can be had upon payment of ten per cent and execution of agreement, whereby the balance is paid in nine half-yearly installments".

Subsequent to that auction, Messrs. Tyser, Greenwood & Crier were involved in marketing the houses built on that site by Mr. H. Jackson of 2 Grove Park Terrace, the development being named the "Riverview Estate", each house being subject to a 99 years lease at Ground Rents of £6. 10s. for the larger houses, and £5. 10s. for the smaller houses, the prices being quoted at £375 and £275 respectively. Furthermore, the vendors were prepared to sell on the basis of only £30 cash, with the balance payable over a period of either ten, or fifteen years.

The development of the residential area in Gordon Road,

Wolseley Gardens and the Burnaby and Whitehall estates led to the erection of a parade of shops between the junction of Sutton Lane with Gordon Road in that part of Sutton Lane which was renamed Fauconberg Road after Baron Fauconberg who had occupied the manor house known as "Sutton Court", with his wife Mary, a daughter of Oliver Cromwell.

During 1905, the Chiswick Adult School was formed and commenced initially at the Mission Hall in Fraser Street, the building erected in 1880 by the Thornycroft employee, Mr. R.T. Smith, but the Adult School removed to the Primitive Methodist School Room in Fishers Lane during 1907, and commenced actively to seek their own premises. However, in 1910, they moved to Kensington House in Turnham Green Terrace, where they remained until 1916 (in the middle of the Great War) and then moved to the Friends Meeting House in Essex Place. The Adult School does not appear to have survived after the Great War of 1914 to 1918.

The Turnham Green National School, which was opened in 1848 on the north side of the High Road, close to Essex Place Square, continued to provide teaching for the infants after the boys department moved out in 1897, but in 1905 Belmont School had opened nearby and the infants were transferred to that school.

Also in 1905, the site of the late eighteenth century "Little Sutton House" on the corner of Sutton Lane and Barrowgate Road, was offered for sale as building land, but the house itself survived until 1924 and in 1928 the premises of "Chiswick Garage" opened on the site.

Another estate of houses was build by Mr. H. Jackson, this time close to the Chiswick Southern Railway Station, on the other side of the railway line from the Grove Park area, and was referred to as the "Orchard Estate". Mr. Jackson established his building yard on the corner of the estate, on the south side of Burlington Lane, just east of the footpath that runs beside the railway line from Chiswick to Barnes Railway Bridge, and Wilmington Avenue was developed.

The houses on that estate were offered for sale by Messrs. Tyser, Greenwood and Company at prices – "from £395, and by payment of a small deposit, tenants may become their own landlords, paying off the balance of the purchase money by installments equivalent to rent, covering various periods from ten years upwards".

As has been mentioned earlier, the Royal Horticultural Society began removing from their Chiswick grounds to Wisley in 1903, and negotiations began shortly afterwards for the lease granted to the Royal Horticultural Society by His Grace, the Duke of Devonshire, in 1870, to be assigned by them to builders by the name of Messrs. Ward & Budd, in 1905. The builders address was originally in Barnes, but they quickly established themselves in Sutton Court Road, Chiswick, and a new building lease was then granted to them by Spencer Compton, then the Duke of Devonshire, commencing on the same date in 1905, whereby His Grace agreed to the proposed purely residential development of the old Horticultural Grounds, with a road running from Sutton Court Road eastwards into Dukes Avenue, named Wavendon Avenue, with two roads running north out of Wavendon Avenue, named Hadley gardens (which turned eastward at a right angle into Dukes Avenue) and Foster Road, which ended into that latter part of Hadley Gardens. The frontage land of that part on the eastern side of Sutton Court Road was also residentially developed, and another road constructed from Sutton Court Road running eastwards into Hadley Gardens, which road was named Alwyn Avenue, and a cul-de-sac turning was created out of the north side of Alwyn Avenue towards Horticultural Place, but not joining it, and that cul-de-sac was named Sharon Road.

All the houses were of the villa type, built either in semi-detached pairs, or in short terraces, mostly with accommodation on two floors, but some at the Dukes Avenue end of Wavendon Avenue, on three floors. The building work was carried out over the subsequent few years and leases granted on each house for a term of ninety-nine years from 25th December 1910, at ground rents of between £7 and £10 per annum. It appears that Alwyn, Foster, Hadley and Sharon are Christian names.

Sutton Court was demolished and in 1905 a block of mansion flats was built on the site which retained the name of Sutton Court.

A residential road was developed in a crescent around the parade of shops in Fauconberg Road and named Hazledene Road, and another residential road was created nearby, between the shops and Sutton Court, turning north out of Fauconberg Road, named Compton Crescent, presumably inspired by the name of the then Duke of Devonshire, Spencer Compton.

Another parade of shops was developed, in 1905 on the north side of the High Road, from the corner of Upham Park Road towards Ennismore Avenue, whilst on the south side of the High Road, just west of Devonshire Road, yet another parade of shops was built, which included number 173, a shop immediately occupied by Mr. Edgar Howard Barnes, a merchant of leather goods, and many years later the shop passed into the hands of his son who expanded the business into hardware goods.

It was probably about 1906 that Messrs. Tyser, Greenwood & Company, as it was by then known, became involved in another estate of houses which Mr. H. Jackson was building, this time advertised as the "Osterley Park Station Estate" and was described on the advertising poster as being "The Healthiest District round London" with "Beautiful walks through Osterley Park and surrounding country". The houses were to be close to the "Electric District Railway, with four trains per hour to and from the City and the West End". Each house had two reception rooms, four bedrooms, bathroom, kitchen and usual offices, and were offered with – "Free Leases at £395, or £45 cash and the balance as moderate rent".

On that poster, no mention was made of the Barnes Office, but Messrs. Tyser, Greenwood & Company's address was still 360 Chiswick High Road, and the branch office at Turnham Green Railway Station was mentioned.

Another builder who became involved in the development of houses in Chiswick, was Mr. G. Marsh, and his development was advertised as the "Little Sutton Estate" which involved the building of a row of houses running from east to west across Sutton Court Road, just south of the Wesleyan Methodist Church and Manse, and those houses were advertised as – "Well built houses . . . containing three and four good bedrooms, etc., . . . electric light, good gardens, at prices from £430 cash, Leasehold at low ground rent, or Freehold at £615".

Thereby Ellesmere and Cedars Roads were created, although subsequently the southern side of both roads were either demolished, or redeveloped, with the buildings set back in order to permit road widening so that the two roads could be included as part of the Cromwell Road and Great West Road dual carriageway extension.

It was in that mid-Edwardian era that Ernest Greenwood became interested in the Letchworth Garden City Estate, then well into being expanded by the First City Ltd., whose registered offices were in London's High Holborn, and whose resident Estate Agent was Mr. W.H. Gaunt. The development of that remarkable new conception was controlled by a Board of Directors with Ralph Neville, K.C., as Chairman and included amongst the other ten directors were Edward Cadbury of Bourneville and others, and the attraction to Londoners was the good railway link from King's Cross Station.

During 1907 a crescent of houses was built in Burlington Lane, opposite to the walled grounds of Chiswick House, between

Corney Road and Grantham Road, and in that same year, some old cottages of wooden construction, close to Castle Place in Back Common Road (later renamed Chiswick Common Road), were demolished and Victor Villas built on the site.

Wakefields, the well known photographers, who had been established in Ealing since 1890, acquired premises during 1908, on the north side of the High Road, immediately east of the early nineteenth century houses and opposite to Airedale Avenue. Also, at about that time, the "Chaffcutter's Arms", a small public house in the High Road, east of Essex Place Square and west of Belmont Road, was closed and that permitted Mr. W. Whiteside to set up his fishmonger's shop on its site, which shop was later taken over by M. R. Portch.

Until 1908, the Jessop family's "Grove Park Farm" extended to the river on the southern side of Burlington Lane, but in that year it was acquired by the Duke of Devonshire.

A young man from Hammersmith, by the name of Ernest Griffen, joined the staff of Messrs. Tyser, Greenwood & Company in about 1908, which staff still included Ernest Parsons, one of Mr. Richard Tyser's staff.

William Soper's store on the north side of the High Road, close to Turnham Green, was acquired, in 1909, by Mr. Percy Goodban and the name of the store was changed to "Goodbans" and retained that name when the business was acquired by Mr. Cecil Cooper and later passed into the hands of his son, Mr. John Cooper, but the store eventually closed in 1974.

During 1908, the Urban District Council of Chiswick decided to go ahead with a scheme to build Open Air Swimming Baths on land which had recently been purchased from His Grace, the Duke of Devonshire, close to Duke's Meadows on the riverside, and the baths were opened in 1910.

Down on Strand-on-the-Green, the old "Ship Inn" closed in 1910, whilst in the High Road, west of the "Windmill", the

"Penny Bazaar" store was opened by Messrs. Marks & Spencer.

Electric cinemas were becoming very popular at that time, and one such cinema opened at 358 Chiswick High Road, next door to the main offices of Messrs. Tyser, Greenwood & Company, and it was named "Palais Cinema" but it closed shortly after the commencement of the Great War, in 1914.

However, on the sixth day of May in 1910, King Edward VII died, to be succeeded by King George V, so the Edwardian era came to an end.

CHAPTER THREE

"King George V and the Post Great War Period"

KING George V succeeded to the throne with Queen Mary, who was a Londoner and thereby very popular with the Londoners.

Although the "Palais Cinema" had closed during the period of the Great War of 1914-1918, another cinema with the name of "Electric Theatre" opened during 1911, on the corner of the High Road with Dukes Road, and that remained until 1933 when the site was redeveloped as a row of four shops.

During the period of 1910 to 1911, the Old Pack Horse, on the corner of Acton Lane and Chiswick High Road, was rebuilt.

The Anglican Sisters of the Order of St. Mary and St. John, who had built, on the advice of Florence Nightingale, the Convent and hospital in Burlington Lane, for handicapped and incurable ladies, amalgamated during 1910, with the Order of St. Margaret.

Another hospital, endowed by Mr. Dan Mason of the Chiswick Polish Company, for the people of Chiswick, was opened in 1910, originally in Burlington Lane, but transferred during the following year to a new building on the riverside at Chiswick Mall beside Rothbury House. That hospital was rebuilt in 1936 but came under national control following the Second World War, and eventually ceased to be a hospital in 1975.

Sir Oswald Stoll completed the erection of the Chiswick Empire, one of a number of his palaces of variety entertainment for the public, and it opened in 1912. The building was on the site he had acquired on the north side of the High Road, overlooking Turnham Green, between the Old Pack Horse and the yard of Caught's, the butcher.

Cullens, the provisions merchants, opened one of their shops in the Chiswick High Road during 1913, followed by other shops spread along what became a lengthy shopping High Road.

Christ Church, Turnham Green, was able to open their Church Hall on the corner of Heathfield Terrace and Heathfield Gardens, shortly before the commencement of the Great War on 4th August 1914, and it was during 1914 that Back Common Road was renamed Chiswick Common Road.

Following the coming into effect of some of the provisions contained within the Finance Act of 1909/1910, there was a sharp decline in the number of residential building being erected, as a result of which it was realised by the Government, upon the outbreak of the Great War, that occupying tenants could be faced with an increase in their rent, or loss of their home, particularly when most of the men-folk would be serving in His Majesty's Forces. Accordingly, an Act of Parliament was hurried through the necessary procedures, entitled "The Rent and Mortgage Interest Restriction Act, 1915", which froze the rents payable on individual houses and flats to the figure payable on the day that the war had been declared, also freezing the interest on mortgage-repayments.

During that war, the lake in the grounds of Grove House was linked to the River Thames by the construction of a canal and a lock, thereby making it possible to convert the lake into a barge building yard for the firm of Holland, Hammer and Cubitts. The barges were constructed of concrete and were used to carry ammunitions to the British Expeditionary Forces in France.

A new Secondary School for girls was being constructed on an open site in Burlington Lane, south of Chiswick House Grounds, and that school was opened during 1916, but the construction of the boys Secondary School on the same site was delayed until 1926, some years after the end of the Great War, during which war something in the order of ten million servicemen were killed.

One of the British new inventions introduced during that war was a vehicle with caterpillar tracks, called a "Tank" and one of those tanks, which had been used by British troops in the war zone, was rescued and positioned on a sloping rockery on the north-west corner of Turnham Green, opposite to the Old Pack Horse, whilst at the other corner of Turnham Green, between Chiswick High Road and Heathfield Terrace, an obelisk was erected as a permanent War Memorial.

Dan Mason, now an established Chiswick philanthropist, acquired "Afton House" in Bourne Place, which had been built during the eighteenth century (when it was known as "Falkland House"), and presented it to the British Legion as the Chiswick Memorial Club for Chiswick's ex-servicemen, and the Club was opened in 1919.

Along with a very great number of other young men throughout the United Kingdom, Ernest Griffen and other members of the staff of Messrs. Tyser, Greenwood & Company, joined His Majesty's Forces and served in the British Expeditionary Forces in France and Belgium. Whereas other staff members found employment elsewhere following the end of that war on 11th November 1918, Ernest Griffen returned to Messrs. Tyser, Greenwood & Company.

The effects arising out of the termination of the Great War of 1914 to 1918 were greater than most people had realised and undoubtedly Messrs. Tyser, Greenwood & Company soon realised that many landlords were seeking their professional advice in respect of the effects of the continuation of rent restriction and statutory protection of tenants. Accordingly, added to their usual main business of Auctioneering and House Agency, also Surveying and Valuations, the management of various properties, particularly residential, increased in volume. The passing of the Rent Restriction Act of 1920 permitted a small increase in the amount of rent which a landlord could impose upon the tenants, but the procedure and the complicated mathematics were not easy for some to comprehend, principally because the majority of residential rents were inclusive of the general and water rates payable on the residents and the percentage increase permitted was based on the "net rent" i.e. after deducting the rates from the amount paid by the tenant.

In the field of house agency there already existed, in Chiswick, a number of competitors to Messrs. Tyser, Greenwood & Company, including Mr. A.J. Fowkes who had an office at number 230 High Road, opposite to the "George IV" public house, also Messrs. Green & Lines who had a small office not far from Caughts, the butcher. However, two brothers returning to civilian life after the Great War, established themselves in quite extensive premises on the southern side of the High Road, adjacent to Prospect Place, on the corner of Heathfield Terrace. The brothers had the surname of "Whitman" and one had become a wartime Colonel and the other a rank of Captain. H.J. Whitman, the Colonel, was principally a builder, whilst his brother was an artistic house and estate agent, and they established a combined firm under the name of "Whitman & Whitman", but some years later the business separated into two distinctly different traders, although the estate agency retained the name of Whitman & Whitman. The corner on which their offices were established became known generally as "Whitman's Corner".

The realisation that there existed a housing shortage in 1914 was even more apparent after at least five years more without active house building, and in 1919, the government endeavoured to rectify the situation by authorising local authorities to acquire land and, for the first time, build residential accommodation to rent to people in need of housing. That was empowered under the Housing Act of 1919.

During that same year, the Chiswick Urban District Council made available two sites for open markets, the principal and the busiest being set back from the south side of the High Road, between Linden Gardens and Devonshire Road, and the other in Essex Place Square.

Memorial Homes for ex-servicemen and their families were provided by Chiswick Charities on land generously donated by His Grace, the Duke of Devonshire, on the southern side of Burlington Lane, not far from the Chiswick Southern Railway Station.

Another outcome of the events which occurred during the Great War, was the establishment of a yacht basin on what had originally been the lake in the grounds of Grove House, used during the war for the building of barges, and for many years afterwards it became known as "Cubitt's Yacht Basin.

The offices of Messrs. Tyser, Greenwood & Company at 360 Chiswick High Road, formed part of an old development and were flanked by other properties suitable for re-development, so during 1921, Ernest Greenwood acquired larger premises at number 386 Chiswick High Road, situated on the western corner of Essex Place Square with a long return frontage to that Square. The whole of the ground floor accommodation and the front section of the upper floor was occupied by Messrs. Tyser, Greenwood & Company, the remaining rear section of the first floor, with a central staircase leading off Essex Place Square, was leased off to a solicitor, Mr. N. Ramsay Murray. The front elevation of the ground floor office, also the front section of the return frontage, comprised oak framed windows of bevelled quarter-plate glass, whilst inside the main entrance office had match-boarded walls and high ceiling. Behind that main, general office was a private office which had a large sash window overlooking Essex

Place Square, and a door giving access to the foot of the stairs which led to Mr. N. Ramsay Murray's offices. Behind that ground floor office were two store rooms, without ceilings other than the underside of the upper flooring, the first store having a single toilet and double-doors to Essex Place Square, and the other store which was larger, had a trap door set in the concrete floor giving access to a cellar, and with brick walls and a further set of double-doors to the Square, also a window, and at the rear a cobble-stoned stable, with a high ceiling and a hay loft, and a large single door to Essex Place Square.

The first floor front offices, occupied by Messrs. Tyser, Greenwood & Company, comprising two quite large offices, each with two sash windows to the front and side elevations respectively, and were reached by means of a straight staircase from the main ground floor general office.

The offices leased to Mr. N. Ramsay Murray were approached by the staircase mentioned, under which there was another trap door giving access to a separated section of the basement store area. At the head of the stairs was one large office to the left of the landing (off which was a toilet), and to the right some smaller partitioned offices running towards the rear, off a corridor along the outer wall flanking Essex Place Square, but the last office, being above the stable and hay loft, was approached up three steps, and the room had a low ceiling.

Messrs. Tyser, Greenwood & Company's old offices at 360 Chiswick High Road, and some adjoining premises, were acquired by F.W. Woolworth for redevelopment as their Chiswick shopping store.

During 1921 and 1922, the London General Omnibus Company created their Chiswick Works on an area of land on the north side of the High Road, opposite to Gunnersbury Railway Station, and stretching back to Bollo Lane, and their works remained there until 1988.

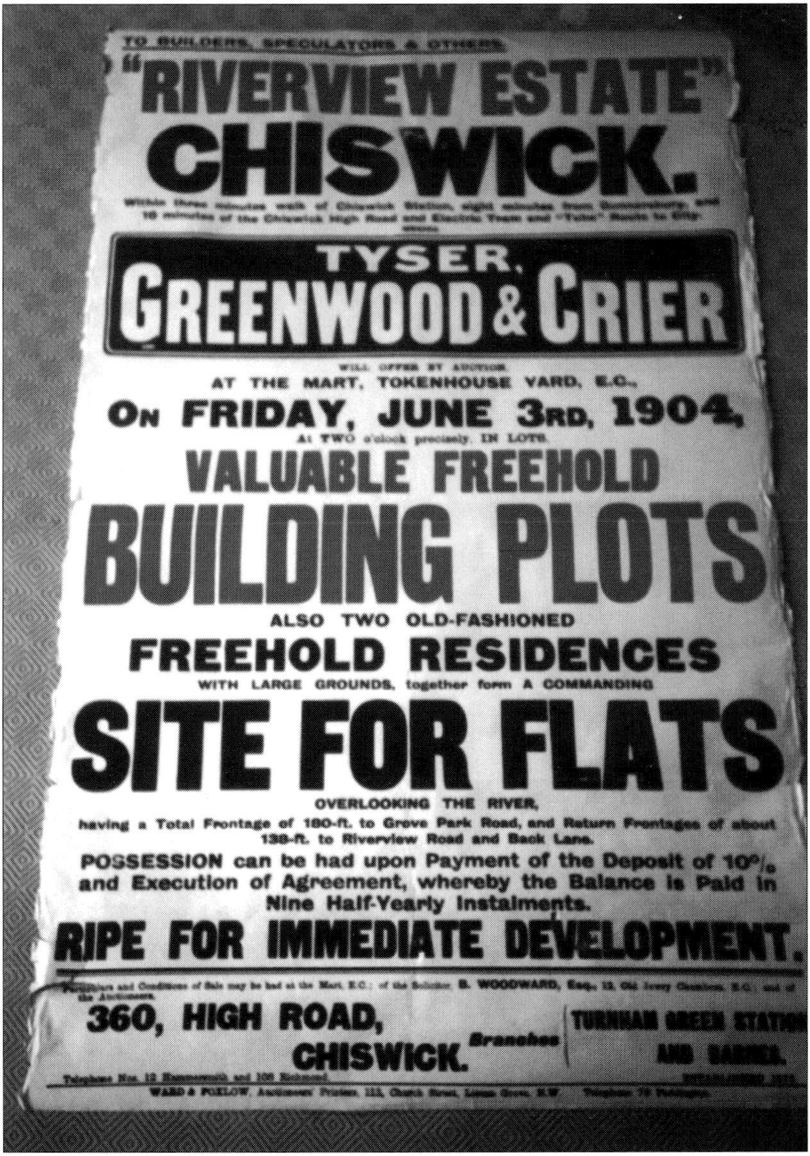

1904 poster of the Riverside Estate Auction

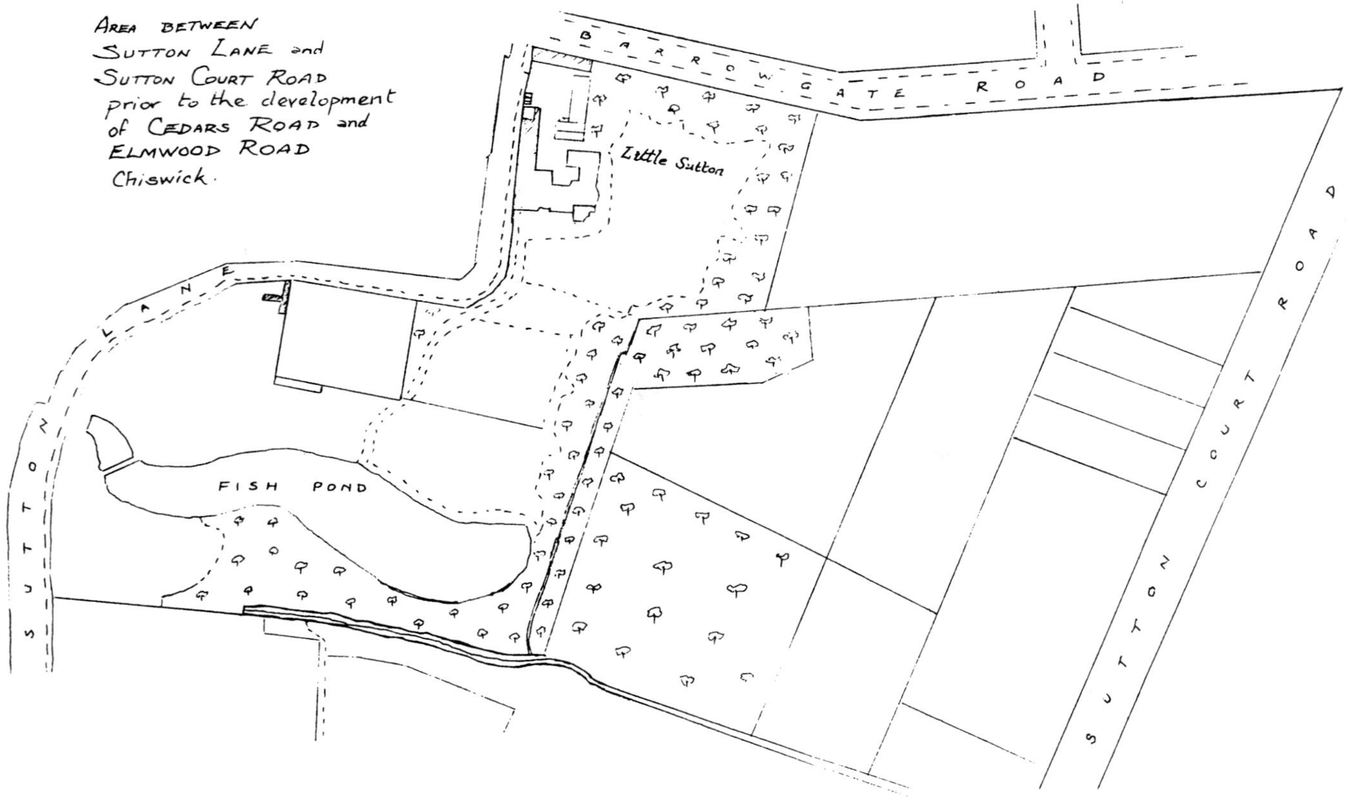

Plan of Little Sutton

MESSRS.

TYSER, GREENWOOD & CO.,

(H. NORMAN HARDING, F.S.I., F.A.I., E. J. GRIFFEN, F.A.I., C. F. LAWES, F.S.I.)

Auctioneers, Valuers, Surveyors and Estate Agents.

Head Office :
386, High Road, Chiswick, W.4.
Telephones : Chiswick 0402, 3, 4.

and at

The Bedford Park Estate Offices,
Turnham Green Station, W.4.
Telephones : Chiswick, 0134, 5.

ESTABLISHED 1873.

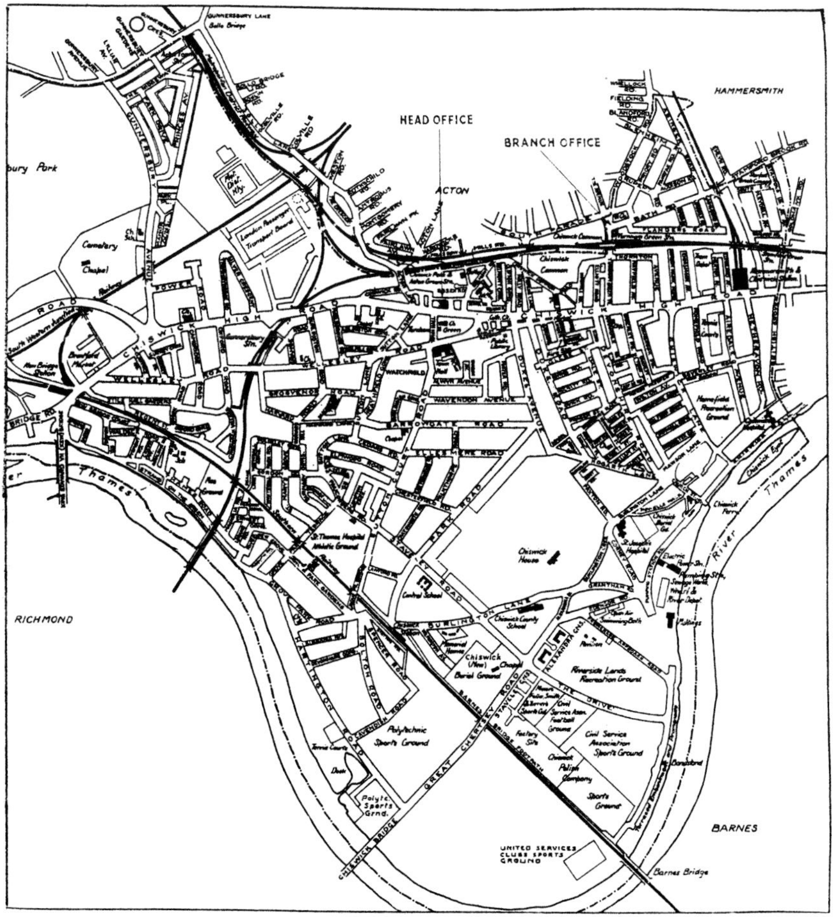

Based upon the Ordnance Survey Map with the Sanction of the Controller of H.M. Stationery Office.

Particulars upon application of available Houses

COLLECTION OF RENTS AND ESTATE MANAGEMENT A SPECIALITY.

Map of Chiswick during 1930's

Dan Mason of the Chiswick Polish Company (Cherry Blossom Polish), bought Boston House in Chiswick Square, opposite to his offices and works which were between Burlington Lane and Hogarth Lane, during 1922, and the house was adapted for use as a club by the female staff members of his Company. Some years later, that Company acquired land at the end of Burlington Lane, beyond Dukes Meadows, and developed houses and flats for members of their staff.

The name of Warwick Draper, a barrister and local historian, has become synonymous with Chiswick, following his writing of the most excellent book entitled "Chiswick" which was published, with the aid of a long list of subscribers, in 1923, at which time Warwick Draper was resident in the eighteenth century "Bedford House" on Chiswick Mall, a house which was built by Edward Russell, son of the fourth Earl of Bedford, during the seventeenth century, and subsequently altered and extended. The list of subscribers to Warwick Draper's book, included His Grace, the Duke of Devonshire; Lt. Col. W. Grant Morgan; Lt. Col. R.W. Shipway; the Rt. Hon. Sir William Bull, a numerous business and tradesmen, as well as local personages, including Mr. Percy L. Fisher, who had become a partner of Ernest Greenwood in the business of Messrs. Tyser, Greenwood & Company.

As mentioned earlier, Ernest Griffen returned to Messrs. Tyser, Greenwood & Company after serving in His Majesty's Forces during the Great War, and not long afterwards a Miss Robinson, the daughter of the editor of the Chiswick Times, became the book-keeper in that firm, and in due course the first recorded office romance led to Miss Robinson becoming Mrs. Ernest Griffen.

The Urban District Council of Chiswick arranged, during 1923, to purchase from His Grace, the Duke of Devonshire, one hundred and fifty acres of riverside land, to which the Council then carried out works such as adapting the embankment for use by the public, and creating shelters and a bandstand, also forming a promenade, part of which was tree lined, and a children's play area, naming the project "Duke's Meadows" and it soon became very well known as it lined part of the University Boat Race and was mentioned over the radio – a new service in the early 1920's – each year.

Another "Bedford House" situated on the northern boundary of Chiswick, and which had formed the centre point of the development of the Bedford Park Garden Suburb in 1875, had its front elevation obscured during 1924, when a parade of shops was built along South Parade and round the corner into The Avenue.

Theatre lovers were delighted when a small theatre opened in 1924, in Kew Bridge Road next door to the Star & Garter Hotel, and which was aptly named the "Q Theatre", but unfortunately lack of support after the Second World War caused it to close in 1956.

By 1925, amongst the new buildings being erected, was one on the corner of the High Road and Belmont Road, for Mr. F.D. Alwright's car hire, car showroom and workshop, a three storey building which dwarfed Mr. W. Whiteside's fishmonger business, next door and probably resulted in him selling to Mr. R. Portch, two years later.

A public house, which could trace its license back to 1706, named the "Queen's Head" in Sutton Lane, close to Harvard Lane (part of the old "Dead Donkey Lane"), was rebuilt in 1925, but the great event of 1925 was the opening, by His Majesty, King George V, of the new road commencing at the western end of the High Road and running westward to relieve the congestion in Brentford's High Street, and better access from the adjacent Brentford Fruit, Flower and Vegetable Market. The road was named "The Great West Road" and was developed into a duel carriageway, with cycle tracks on either side, the first section of which became a commercial centre known as "The Golden Mile".

The open market which existed just off the High Road,

between Devonshire Road and Linden Gardens, had become the subject of numerous complaints from the Chiswick residents, so the Council decided to build an indoor market behind the open market, with an extra exit in Linden Gardens, and move the traders into those premises. The indoor market opened in 1926 but it proved to be unpopular with the traders and by 1937 the premises were used to rehouse the fire services which had occupied the nearby premises with the predominant clock tower since 1891. The fire service remained there until a new fire station was built in 1963, at the corner of Heathfield Gardens and Sutton Lane.

The premises with the clock tower vacated by the fire services, were occupied by the electrical installers owned by the local authority who encouraged occupiers of all properties within their area to install and use electricity, by offering very favourable terms. Small houses could be wired and supplied with electricity for as little as six old pennies per week, and at least one small house, in Glebe Street is known to have had rejected gas lighting in favour of oil lamps, but were persuaded to convert to electricity a few years before the commencement of the Second World War, in 1939.

Whereas girls had been provided with a Secondary Education School in 1915, on an open site in Burlington Lane, close to the southern boundary of Chiswick House Grounds, work at last commenced on building an extension to that school to provide for boy pupils. That extension was completed and opened in 1927.

Grove House, which had been the walled home of the Earl of Grantham, contained within its grounds which extended to the River Thames, a lake which became the Cubitt's Yacht Basin following the First World War, all became within the ownership of His Grace, the Duke of Devonshire, but the Grove House itself, with its immediate garden land, had become the home of Col. R.W. Shipway, J.P.

Bolton Road and Spencer Road, both running southward from the Grove Park Hotel, already had some fine Victorian Houses, including one erected in Bolton Road during 1887, which became Mrs. Crampton's Ladies College, but which was later converted into two separate houses and became known as numbers one and two Devonshire Gardens, a new road running east towards the river.

Some more fine late Victorian houses had been built in a road named Hartington Road, after the courtesy title of the first son of the Duke of Devonshire, running from Grove Park Road to the riverside sports grounds, and the houses built on the west side of that road, had long gardens running down to the river. Another road, named after the Duke's family name, Cavendish Road, was constructed to link the southern end of both Bolton and Spencer Roads to Hartington Road. The Quinton Hogg Memorial Sports Ground occupied the land on the south side of Cavendish Road.

For a while, during the early post First World War years, Chiswick House and Grounds were used as a private asylum for the mentally ill, but in 1928, the House and grounds were purchased by the Middlesex County Council, with a contribution from His Majesty, King George V (who had fond memories of Chiswick House and Grounds during his boy-hood days), to provide a public park.

During October 1928 Chiswick experienced one of its greatest fires when the Sanderson Wallpaper Factory, in Barley Mow Passage, went up in flames. Fortunately there was no loss of life, but the factory became unusable and the fire caused damage to the adjacent Chiswick Public Library.

Mr. Ernest Greenwood and his partner, Mr. Percy Fisher (who had become a Life Vice-President of the British Amateur Athletic Association) were continuing their practice of Messrs. Tyser, Greenwood & Company, and in 1928 they took into their employment, a young lad by the name of Ernest Simpson, who had received training as a short-hand typist and book-keeper, and he was placed at the firm's Bedford Park Office. The following year another young lad was employed at the main Chiswick Office, by the name of George Bradley, upon the transfer of a more senior staff member who was put in charge of the Bedford Park Office. Both the new employees recall that Percy Fisher was prone to sleeping sickness and could be found asleep in his first floor office, so it was necessary to knock loudly on the door of his office in order to ensure he would awake before they entered.

George Bradley remembers being very impressed by Mr. Ernest Greenwood who he described as being a tall, imposing "Victorian" gentleman, not given to being very generous, and who had the habit of looking over the top of his spectacles. He also recalls that by about mid-morning, Ernest Greenwood and Percy Fisher would get together and Ernest Greenwood would telephone the "Star & Garter Hotel" at the foot of Kew Bridge by the fountain, to ascertain what was on the menu for lunch that day, and then they would discuss what they would order before adjourning for their lunch at that hotel.

The "Star & Garter Hotel" became the meeting place of the local Rotary Club, which contrary to the alphabetical order of Brentford & Chiswick which was chosen by the Council, instead used the name of the Chiswick & Brentford Rotary Club.

Another recollection of George Bradley is that Ernest Greenwood used an Alvis motor car to reach the office from his home in Ealing, sometimes driving himself, but sometimes being driven by one of his daughters, generally Kathleen, who also became a part-time book-keeper at both the Chiswick and Bedford Park Offices.

At that time, members of the staff were expected to apply, in writing, to Ernest Greenwood if they thought that they warranted a rise in salary, and invariably their letter would remain, presumably unopened, on Ernest Greenwood's desk.

The inter-war years of economic depression resulted in the execution of public works in the latter years of the 1920's, including the widening of Gunnersbury Lane and following completion of the work, in 1931, the roadway was renamed Gunnersbury Avenue. Some new building of houses commenced a few years after the Great War, and in Chiswick this appears to have started in spaces alongside existing residential development in existing roads. The style of the houses were quite different from the houses erected in the Edwardian era, which themselves differed from the Victorian houses. The tendencies were towards smaller houses with smaller, less lofty, rooms; electric light replaced gas lighting, although gas supply was still installed for cooking purposes, and for the first time in good class dwellings, no provision was made for a resident servant.

By the year 1921 the population of Chiswick exceeded forty thousand people and it was realised by the Council that there would be need for another secondary education school. Accordingly, some land on the north side of Burlington Lane was acquired, just east of Chiswick Southern Railway Station and west of the existing County School, on the southern side of Burlington Lane. The new school was built fronting a new road which ran between Sutton Court Road and Burlington Lane, named Staveley Road, with its own sports grounds reaching back to Burlington Lane, and was opened in 1927.

New house development had commenced on the surrounding land, all of which had originally been part of the Chiswick Park Farm, and some of the houses were supplied with a garage for housing the family car. The names given to the roads created for those houses were associated with the Freeholder, His Grace, the Duke of Devonshire, such as Chesterfield Road (linking Sutton Court Road with Park Road) with the houses on the northern side set well back to avoid the Bollo Brook underground; Eastbourne, Milnthorpe, Chatsworth and Lawford Roads. Staveley Road itself had young flowering cherry trees planted on both sides of the carriageway, which provided a very attractive sight in the Spring of each year, and it is believed that Queen Mary was always delighted to make a trip to see the trees in full bloom.

During 1931 and 1932, the Underground District Railway Station known as Chiswick Park Station, just north of the High Road in Acton Lane, was rebuilt.

Also in 1932, a Campanile was added to the Roman Catholic Church of Our Lady of Grace and Saint Edwards, as a memorial to the Roman Catholics from Chiswick who were killed during the Great War, which later became known as the First World War.

Possibly as a result of the opening of the Great West Road in 1925, and the creation of the "Golden Mile", previously mentioned, the Urban District Councils of both Brentford and Chiswick endeavoured to join together to form a Borough, and those endeavours resulted in the granting of the Royal Charter of Incorporation for the creation of the Borough of Brentford & Chiswick, and a great celebration took place on 18th October 1932. The two Urban District Councils had agreed that the Charter Mayor should be Mr. James Clements, who had been the Chairman of the Brentford District Council in 1903, and as such was present when His Majesty, King Edward VII had formally opened the bridge across the River Thames, which bears his name but which has always been referred to as "Kew Bridge".

For those 1932 celebrations, a Mayoral procession was organised whereby the High Sheriff of Middlesex, Lt. Col. M.F.M.S. Kittoe, who represented His Majesty, King George V, was met at Kew Bridge from whence the procession made its way to Turnham Green for the ceremony of handing over the Royal Charter to the Charter Mayor.

The procession was enlarged during the afternoon, by the inclusion of decorated carts and lorries, proceeding around the whole borough, finishing at Boston Manor Park, and during the evening a great gathering of people indulged in Community singing, followed by a stupendous fireworks display.

Mr. Percy Fisher, in his capacity of Life Vice-Chairman of the Amateur Athletic Association, absented himself from the offices of Messrs. Tyser, Greenwood & Company, on special athletic occasions, from time to time, sometimes travelling overseas, and on one such occasion (it is believed to have been the British Empire Games), in 1932, he died quite unexpectedly. The effect of that death on Mr. Ernest Greenwood was devastating and doubtless the effects of the economic recession being experienced at that same time, affected Mr. Greenwood's thinking, but in any event he decided to take early retirement and to seek someone to acquire the practice of his firm. In the meantime he wished to safeguard the livelihood of a faithful member of the staff, Mr. Ernest Griffen, who had served the firm from before the First World War, and had subsequently qualified as an Associated Member of the Chartered Auctioneers & Estate Agents Institute. The practice of Messrs. Tyser, Greenwood & Company was acquired, principally, by a young man of some stature, the son of a wine merchant living in the Isleworth-Osterley area, and who had been educated at Stowe and St. Paul's School, followed by becoming an articled pupil to Sir Howard Frank of Messrs. Knight, Frank & Rutley of Hanover Square. During the First World War, this young man served with distinction in the Westminster Dragoons and was awarded the Military Cross, finishing the war with the full rank of Major. During his military service he developed an affection for a young American nurse, so upon his return to Messrs. Knight, Frank & Rutley, he persuaded Sir Howard Frank to assign him to an appointment in the United States of America in order to marry his American Nurse.

That young man was Henry Norman Harding, and following the war he undertook the necessary examinations to qualify as a member of the Surveyors Institution and he was duly elected as a

Fellow of that Institution on 6th December 1926, and subsequently he also became a Fellow of the Chartered Auctioneers & Estate Agents Institute.

Having decided to acquire the practice of Messrs. Tyser, Greenwood & Company from Ernest Greenwood, Norman Harding (as he was always known generally) found it necessary to seek another partner (apart from Ernest Griffen) and that proved to be another Chartered Surveyor, Mr. Cecil Lawes, who was put in charge of the firm's Bedford Park office, whilst Ernest Griffen remained, with the new senior partner, at the main Chiswick offices.

Another young lad, who had just completed his secondary school education, was then employed in a junior position, at the Bedford Park Offices, and his name was Eric Morton, who lived with his maiden aunt in Bath Road, close to that office.

In addition to the residential development already mentioned on the site of the Jessop's family "Chiswick Park Farm", the demolition of "Grove House" on the other side of the railway line, took place during 1928, followed by the Kinnaird Property Company carrying out residential redevelopment of the site with new dwellings in that part of Grove Park Road, and the creation of Kinnaird Avenue and Devonshire Gardens, both linked to Hartington Road.

During the early 1930's, the demolition of a large house at the Turnham Green end of Sutton Court Road, known as "Watchfield House" took place and on its site a block of flats was erected which retained the name of "Watchfield Court".

Also, in Hartington Road, a block of flats was built between some existing houses and the riverside Boat Club, and that block was named "Hartington Court".

Some newer houses had been built in both Bolton and Spencer Roads, also a few in Cavendish Road, facing the Polytechnic Sports Grounds, and in addition, a small block of residential flats, named "Kelvin Court" was built in Spencer Road.

During 1932, another new main road was about to be created by the commencement of the construction of new bridges at Chiswick and Twickenham, and the new road which was named the "Great Chertsey Road", commenced in Burlington Lane, just outside the main gates of Chiswick House, and swept through the riverside sports grounds crossing the River Thames just beyond the termination point of the University Boat Race, opposite to the Mortlake Brewery, then on to Richmond, forming a round-about at the end of Kew Road, and over the second new bridge and the St. Margarets area of Twickenham, and proceeding to Chertsey. Following completion of the works, in 1933, the road was formally opened by His Royal Highness, the Prince of Wales, who became the uncrowned King Edward VIII.

The Fromow family had been associated with Chiswick since William Fromow of Norfolk decided, in 1829, to establish his nursery business just south-west of Turnham Green, on the corner of Sutton Lane and Wellesley Road, where it flourished and remained until heavy death duties became payable in the early 1930's, whereupon the family sold that site for residential development, resulting in three blocks of flats being built which were named Beverley, Belgrave and Beaumont Courts. The little parade of shops opposite to that development, between Walpole Gardens and Wellesley Road, retained the name of "Fromow's Corner". The Fromow's nursery transferred to a site immediately south of the District Railway Line, close to Chiswick Park Station, on the east side of Acton Lane.

Despite the apparent affluence of new development, the first years of the 1930's were economically precarious following the collapse of the stock market in the United States of America's Wall Street during 1929, which eventually led to Great Britain suspending payments in gold, following similar action by a dozen other nations, and ultimately the United States of America.

In those circumstances, it was not surprising when, late in

1933, the author's father had an accident that threatened to cause him to become incapacitated for the rest of his life, that his only son should have his education interrupted and be forced to seek gainful employment. At that time, the Borough of Brentford & Chiswick had a Juvenile Employment Officer by the name of Ernest Reekie, and it was he who decided that young William P. Roe, despite being younger than most secondary education school leavers, would probably be suitable for the position of office boy at the Chiswick offices of Messrs. Tyser, Greenwood & Company. Accordingly, he arranged for an interview with the partners of that firm and the event is clearly remembered by the author, who entered those offices with a note of introduction, and was asked to sit on the long oak bench that occupied the outer wall of the ground floor general office, together with a pair of upright oak chairs, at the foot of the flight of stairs leading to the upper floor. Within a few minutes, a gentleman wearing a brown suit and with large brown eyes, came out of the private office at the rear of the general office, to say that the author wouldn't be kept waiting long. That gentleman turned out to be Ernest Griffen, and when called into the private office, the author found himself confronted by an imposing, large baldheaded man who was the senior partner H. Norman Harding. A number of questions were put by both partners, the details of which cannot be recalled, but the author was then directed to a smaller desk, in the corner of the private office, and given a piece of paper and a pen and requested to write a letter of application for the position of office boy.

The author was quite happy to comply until he made reference to having available, for their inspection should they so wish, all his school reports during his school career. The problem was – how to spell the word "career" and the word finished up being spelt "carier" which was patently wrong. Upon the partners reading the letter it became obvious that they also thought the word was not correctly spelt, but neither seemed to know the correct spelling either, so Ernest Griffen dashed out of the office and went upstairs to the senior short-hand typist, a Miss Pauline Ellerton, who gave the correct spelling. The incident must have been quite amusing to the partners, who informed me that they would let me know shortly, and a few days later a letter arrived from the senior partner, offering the author a job at a commencing salary of twelve shillings and sixpence per week, commencing on Monday 14th January 1934.

Apart from some six and a half years serving in His Majesty's Forces throughout the Second World War, the author remained with Messrs. Tyser, Greenwood & Company until he retired at the end of March 1985.

As office boy, my duties included answering the telephone and by means of the firm's private exchange switch-board, put the calls through to the person asked for by the caller, or to someone who could answer their enquiries. Apart from the two partners already mentioned, there was, at that time, an office manager, Mr. W. Inge, who was due to leave and join a relative in business elsewhere; Mr. J.W. Clough who was destined to become the office manager; two other young gentlemen, George S. Bradley (who I knew as a senior at my school and as the brother of one of my sister's friends) and Len Pays, both with their own desk in the general office; also the tall lad who had been the office boy prior to my arrival, John Stripp.

In the offices upstairs there were two short-hand typists and the full time book-keeper, Miss Mary M. Gosling, who was assisted on a part-time basis by Miss Kathleen Greenwood; plus someone who appeared to be quite elderly, Ernest Parsons, who's principal duties seemed to be the collection of rents for the considerable number of clients who's properties the firm managed on their behalf, not the least of which was Ernest Greenwood, and to oversee the repairs necessary from time to time to those properties.

There was yet another person employed by Messrs. Tyser,

Greenwood & Company, and his name was Ted Clapton, who had a bicycle on which he transported the firm's flag boards to and from various local properties, proclaiming that the property was either "For Sale" or "To Be Let" or "Sold", as the case may be, also to deliver urgent local letters and to "billpost" the periodic auction posters on a number of local billboards. Ted Clapton supplemented his wages by playing the piano and/or his own accordion at various functions, in the evenings, or at weekends.

In those days, Ernest Parsons lived in one of the short parade of shops with living accommodation, in Acton Lane just behind the "Packhorse", known as Chiswick Terrace, which formed part of the properties immediately around the "Chiswick Empire" which was owned by Sir Oswald Stoll. Ernest Parsons was the first one in Chiswick Terrace and the shop part was used by his two sons, one as a builders supplies merchant, and the other as a general builder, who employed a couple of workmen, and that son drove a Vauxhall car.

It was from that shop that the staff members were able to obtain the keys to the Chiswick office, and return them in the evening, although Ernest Parsons was nearly always the first at the office, before opening time, and he included in his duties the task of sweeping the entrance porch and the pavement in front of the office.

Seniority of staff, in those days, was strictly recognised and adhered to, hence the senior and junior short-hand typists, and the position of the staff members in the general office, with the junior clerk, John Stripp, positioned close to the entrance door, then Len Pays, then George Bradley, then the manager, with the office boy tucked at the back of the office, behind the manager, and close to the private telephone exchange which was situated in a cupboard under the staircase.

Not long after commencing his employment as office boy, the author answered a telephone call from a gentleman who wished to speak to Ernest Griffen and when asked for his name the gentleman replied "The Earl of Grove Park". Suitably impressed, I informed Mr. Griffen of the call only to be met with a great burst of laughter, and it transpires that the "Earl of Grove Park" was a Mr. Arthur E. Hyams, a Certified Bailiff, who had a small estate agency office within the curtilage of Chiswick Southern Railway Station, facing the junction of Sutton Court Road with Burlington Lane.

Another reason for the office boy to be positioned at the rear of the general office was because H. Norman Harding, the senior partner, had a bell push beside his desk and when he rang that bell the office boy, or in his absence another member of staff, had to hasten to his office to discover what he required which quite often was another packet of cigarettes to be purchased from the nearby tobacconist.

Both Norman Harding and Ernest Griffen were prolific smokers, a habit which most men who served in the forces during the Great War of 1914 to 1918 had acquired.

Despite the fact that smoking was so prevalent, it was not permitted in the general office during office hours, which resulted in those members of staff who were "hooked" on smoking, to control their habit to those times when they were able to escape from the office, which fortunately for them was fairly frequently as their tasks included inspecting properties that came onto the market, also to accompany interested people over those properties. An alternative was for them to resort to the toilet facilities at the rear of the office, access to which the staff were required to carry a key to the side door off Essex Place Square.

Practically every member of the general office staff aimed to become qualified either as a practicing member of the Auctioneers & Estate Agents Institute, or the Surveyors Institution, and the staff members achieved that by attending evening classes and, in due course, take the examination leading up to qualification. As the author had left school sooner than had been expected, he had not obtained examination qualifications which would have exempt him from taking the preliminary examination, so his first task was to enlist for evening classes and in due course take the preliminary examination, which was achieved early in 1936.

During 1934, the Hammersmith & Chiswick Riverside Preservation Committee was formed, which included a number of famous artists and authors who were resident along the Hammersmith Mall and Terrace and Chiswick Mall, and that led to the Borough of Brentford & Chiswick putting forward to the Minister of Health, a town-planning scheme to preserve the nature of its part of that riverside area and schedule it as a residential area to prevent the return of any industrial, or commercial uses.

During May of 1935, the Silver Jubilee of His Majesty King George V and Queen Mary was celebrated with great events including a Thanksgiving Service at St. Paul's Cathedral with crowd lined processions to and from that service, followed with subsequent drives by the Royal Couple in other parts of London, the nearest to Chiswick being Hammersmith Broadway on 8th June 1935. Sir Oswald Stoll produced a Jubilee Programme for the Chiswick Empire to cover the 6th May celebrations, and the programme included Ella Shields and G.H. Elliott, who were followed during the next week by the Crazy Gang.

Most unfortunately, His Majesty, King George V died shortly afterwards, on 20th January 1936, and his state funeral procession took place on 29th January. His Royal Highness, the Prince of Wales, was proclaimed King Edward VIII but he abdicated on 11th December in favour of his brother, the Duke of York, who was crowned King George VI with Queen Elizabeth (the Queen Mother to be) in May 1937.

For some years the inhabitants of Chiswick had enjoyed seeing the Royal Family, and a whole host of high class vehicles passing along the Chiswick High Road on their way to Windsor Castle, or to the Ascot Races in the summer months.

During the author's early days with Messrs. Tyser, Greenwood & Company he gained the impression that the London County Council had become envious of the considerable commercial popularity of the "Golden Mile" and the Great West Road which had been opened in 1925. In any event, the London County Council devised a plan to reach the Great West Road without having to resort to the rather devious journey around Hammersmith Broadway and along King Street and Chiswick High Road.

The plan was to widen the existing Cromwell Road, south of Hammersmith Road and St. Paul's School, and to create a dual carriageway road just north of the River Thames, but the boundary of the London County Council terminated at British Grove which lay within the Borough of Brentford & Chiswick and the County of Middlesex. Never-the-less, it took an Act of Parliament, the Trunk Road Act of 1936 to empower the London County Council, also the Minister of Transport, to make the purchases, by compulsion if necessary, of all properties along the route of that proposed dual carriageway, which would slice through British Grove, Netheravon Road, Airedale Avenue, across the Homefields Playing fields, eliminate Mawson Lane, widen Hogarth Lane on the side of the "New Chiswick Town"estate (the properties within that estate having been declared unfit and were due for demolition), cutting across the southern end of Dukes Avenue and the northern end of Park Road; widening Ellesmere and Cedars roads, on the northern side, including the demolition of a few houses in Sutton Court Road, and continuing across the top of Harvard Hill and demolishing the southern side of that section of Harvard Road; over the railway and Wellesley Road, Oxford and Cambridge Roads; eliminating Stonehill Road and much of Surrey Crescent, in order to join up with the Great West Road.

The cries of the local residents that the proposed works would effectively slice Chiswick in half fell on deaf ears, so both the London County Council and the Ministry of Transport commenced their respective issuing of compulsory purchase notices.

It was realised by Norman Harding and his partners in Messrs. Tyser, Greenwood & Company, that all the properties required by the Minister of Transport were within the Chiswick area, and that the Minister would probably require local managing agents to handle the properties, as and when purchased, so appropriate representations were made by Norman Harding and Ernest Griffen, which included a visit to the offices of the Ministry of Transport, resulting in Messrs. Tyser, Greenwood & Company being duly appointed as their managing agents.

Readers are reminded that the majority of residential property continued to be tenant occupied, rather than owner occupied, during those inter-war years, the effect of the Rent Restriction Acts still having considerable influence. Further-more, it was quite common for a vacant house to be offered "To be Let or Sold" as the value of the house was the same whether the house was let to a good tenant, or vacant. Accordingly, most of the houses being purchased by the Ministry throughout Chiswick were occupied by tenants, and the local authorities were given the task of providing alternative accommodation. Not surprisingly, some of the occupiers found their own alternative accommodation from amongst those houses and flats being offered "To be Let".

During the period until the tenants found alternative accommodation, the houses had to be managed and the rents collected and accounted for in the usual manner, but when the houses became vacant all the services (gas, electricity and water) were disconnected, and the properties secured against unlawful entry by ripping up the flooring within the house and using the timber to board up the doors and windows.

On those properties which had been boarded up posters were displayed declaring that "ALL TRESPASSERS would be PROSECUTED by order of Messrs. Tyser, Greenwood & Co."

Mr H. Norman Harding found himself involved as Executor of the will of the owner of Heston House, a Mr. Fenton, in the need to arrange the sale of all the considerable contents of the House, and subsequently the House itself, and that occurred during the latter months of 1936.

As a great advocate of auction sales, Norman Harding arranged for most of the late Mr. Fenton's effects to be disposed of by auction as he considered that such gave a clear indication that every opportunity had been given to anyone wishing to purchase and thereby the best possible price was obtained.

Accordingly, Norman Harding became much respected as an auctioneer, and he became personally involved with the London Auction Mart in the City, and Messrs. Tyser, Greenwood & Company regularly hired one of the rooms at the Mart at their Queen Victoria Street premises. Never-the-less, most of the local properties were auctioned at the general office at 386 Chiswick High Road, which was named "The Auction Sale Room".

During the 1930's, it was customary for each district to have a recognised "early closing day", and in Chiswick that was a Thursday, which resulted in Messrs. Tyser, Greenwood & Company's offices being very quiet on a Thursday afternoon, therefore any local Auction Sale took place on a Thursday evening, so that the general office could be cleared and rearranged for the Auction, during the quiet afternoon.

Partners and staff would then retire to the local "ABC" (Aerated Bread Company) who had tea rooms at number 300 Chiswick High Road, on the corner of Holly Road, before returning to be ready for the Auction Sale.

The office manager in those days was a Mr. R.W.J. Clough, who qualified, in due course, as a Chartered Surveyor, and another office romance resulted in the senior short-hand typist, Miss Pauline Ellerton, becoming Mrs. Clough. R.W.J. Clough left to form his own business, as did George Bradley who joined the staff of a City firm, resulting in the appointment of a new office manager, a Mr. Maurice W. Martin. Another new member of the staff, at about that time, was Victor Stroud, whose father was a local Councillor and who subsequently became an Alderman of the Borough of Brentford & Chiswick. In addition, Eric Morton, who was employed at the Bedford Park Office, was transferred to the Chiswick office, and the author then discovered that they shared the same birthday, that being discovered during the rigid procedure undertaken to ensure that the considerable amount of cash that had been collected in the office during the latter part of the day, was deposited in the "wall night safe" of the Westminster Bank at 314 Chiswick High Road, on the corner of Clifton Gardens. The cash and cheques were placed in one, or two, leather wallets issued by the bank, which had to be deposited into the banks wall safe, and the procedure was that two alert young men would together take those wallets for deposit, shortly before the office closed, but always at varying times each evening. During one of these journeys the author and Eric Morton discovered that despite a difference of three years, their common birthday was being celebrated on the following day.

The author recalls that during the 1930's, the homes of many working class people were confined either to small, cottage type, houses comprising two rooms upstairs and two downstairs, with an outside toilet, or part of a slightly larger, generally terrace, house, probably three rooms with shared amenities. Some such homes were kept clean and reasonably comfortable, but some tenants allowed their homes to become sordid and unhealthy. Despite the passing of years, two such tenants, living literally around the corner from each other, the one a hard working couple with several children occupying the upper three rooms of a small house, managed extreamly well with their one large room occupied as a dormitory; whereas a miserable man and his wife occupied the ground floor rooms of a similar house, somehow allowed those rooms to become filthy and unkempt, and they had one daughter who eventually became pregnant as a result of the drunken fathers abuse.

In another instance a small house, in another part of Chiswick, was occupied by a man and his wife, who by the age of thirty-eight had given birth to thirteen children, and neither husband or wife were often found at home, the mother apparently frequented a local public house, and the children were frequently fed by kindly neighbours.

During 1936, a new block of flats named "Heathfield Court" was built on the south side of Turnham Green, on the site of numbers three to nine Heathfield Terrace, on the corner of Horticultural Place.

Although, in those days, no-one was allowed to vote in either Local Authority or General Elections until they reached the age of twenty-one, never-the-less the author and his colleague, Eric Morton, followed the proceedings of the Parliamentary Election that took place in 1936, and together attended a rally during the evening and well into the night, held at the Albert Hall, when a strong Conservative Government was returned, and the Member for Brentford and Chiswick was Mr. Harold Mitchell. He remained the Member of Parliament for Brentford & Chiswick for many years including the whole of the period of the Second World War, and his name has been given to the new development of the Brentford, Chiswick & Isleworth Conservative Head Quarters in Chiswick High Road.

As has been mentioned earlier, the great occasion during 1937, was the Coronation of Their Majesties, King George VI and Queen Elizabeth in May of that year.

Some events that were occurring in Europe were beginning to

cause concern to the Government of Neville Chamberlain, but he resolutely endeavoured to follow the route of peaceful existence. A meeting took place in Munich on 29th September 1938, between Chamberlain of Great Britain; Daladier of France also Mussolini of Italy, with Adolf Hitler of Germany, in order to achieve a peaceful solution to the problem that Hitler maintained existed over Czechoslovakia. Neville Chamberlain returned to Britain proclaiming "Peace in our Time" but, never-the-less, during the latter months of that year workmen commenced digging up parts of Turham Green close to the War Memorial, in order to construct public Air Raid Shelters.

When, in 1875, Jonathan T. Carr planned the garden suburb of Brentford Park, he arranged for one church, St. Michaels & All Angels; one public house, the Tabard; and one community centre in the form of the Bedford Park Club, in the Avenue. Whereas the club had been well supported for many years after it was opened at the end of the nineteenth century, having a strong appeal to the many actors, musicians and artists who found the environment of Bedford Park most congenial, including one well known actor, Ronald Colman, who became universally famous as a film star in the 1920's and 1930's, who first acted on the stage of the Club. Never-the-less, there began a decline during the difficult years of the 1930's, and in the event, when the Second World War commenced on 3rd September 1939, the Club was closed and both the premises, which were beside Bedford House in The Avenue, and the contents, were offered for sale by Auction. The sale of the contents took place on 20th November 1939, Mr. H. Norman Harding of Messrs. Tyser, Greenwood & Company being the Auctioneer, and items sold included a grand pianoforte; five Brussel's tapestry panels; a full sized billiard table; a George III silver punch bowl; numerous chairs and tables, as well as pictures and mirrors.

CHAPTER FOUR

"The main shopping area of Chiswick High Road in the Mid-1930's"

WHEN I joined Messrs. Tyser, Greenwood & Company as a very junior office boy in 1934, Chiswick High Road was a renowned shopping centre to which people flocked from many other, more outlying suburbs, and which the people of Chiswick used extensively, although in those days, a real venture into the world of shopping involved catching the number twenty-seven 'bus to Kensington where there was a choice of at least three enormous, multi-storied, stores that sold almost everything – Pontings, Barkers and Derry & Toms.

Until 1935, trams ran along their tracks in the centre of Chiswick High Road, supplied with electric power from the Power House adjacent to the tram depot which was situated on the north side of the High Road, beyond Chiswick Lane and before Young's Corner, where some of the trams (I believe it was those numbered fifty-seven) turned into Goldhawk Road and terminated at Shepherds Bush Green.

In opposition to the trams were the motor 'buses run by the General Omnibus Company who had extensive works, also on the north side of the High Road, but in the other direction, immediately opposite to Gunnersbury Railway Station; also a 'bus garage in Belmont Road where scores of 'buses were housed overnight, and which made "Turnham Green" a renowned terminus with late night 'buses providing transport home for Chiswick people into the early hours of the morning, as well as early morning 'buses for the workers who lived in Chiswick.

During 1935, the old trams were replaced by electricity driven trolley 'buses, which obtained their power from a pair of overhead cables and so they did not have to adhere to the metal tracks in the centre of the road, as did the trams, and so they were able to manoeuvre to the curbside for picking up and setting down passengers. In that manner they were able to compete with the petrol driven motor 'buses, but the trolley 'bus drivers had to be extremely careful how they manoeuvred around corners otherwise one or other of their arms flew off the overhead cables thus leaving the trolley 'bus without the power supply, other than their reserve battery, for such an emergency. Another disadvantage, was that they could not pass each other, a fact which resulted in a string of trolley 'buses following the slowest driver.

By 1936, the clanging sound of the old trams could no longer be heard, and with the aid of Kelly's Street Directory and my own memory, I can take a stroll along the busiest section of Chiswick High Road.

Messrs. Tyser, Greenwood & Company's offices are situated on the corner of Essex Place Square, opposite to Christ Church on Turnham Green, and in those days, the Square was a public meeting place and somewhere for all and sundry to come and perform, or address the passing crowds on political, or other matters. As the Square also provided the main entrance and exit for Whitbread's Bottling Plant, the crowds that gathered would have to give way when one of that brewer's many delivery vehicles wished to enter, or leave. Although, by then, most of those vehicles were lorries fitted with internal combustion engines, never-the-less, there were frequent visits by large carts pulled by magnificent shire horses.

On the other corner of Essex Place Square was a gents outfitters trading under the name of "John Bright", and behind it, flanking the Square, was one of the old National Schools. Another National School was situated on the southern side of Turnham Green, on the corner of Heathfield Terrace and Horticultural Place, one for boys and the other for girls.

Next to John Bright's was Joel's (Fruit) Ltd., and next to them W. Barratt & Company's shoe and boot retailers shop, and then at number 378, was R. Portch, a long established wet fish shop.

Number 376 was on the corner of Belmont Road, and those premises were occupied by F.W. Allwright's motor car show room, with repairs garage along the flank and at the rear, stretching back to Essex Place, a passageway where, in those days, there existed a few cottages still occupied as homes.

The Turnham Green 'Bus Garage in Belmont Road has already been mentioned, and on the other side is the Belmont Road School, which presumably replaced the two National Schools a generation earlier. As an infant I attended the Belmont Road School in 1923. On the other corner of Belmont Road with the High Road is the public house named The Crown & Anchor, and next to it was one of David Grieg's provisions shops; then Nofar Ltd. (milliners), followed by Mumby & Company, tailors at number 368; then Miss Shier, tobacconist; A. Anderson, ladies tailors; Kendall & Sons, umbrellas, followed by F.W. Woolworth's stores which occupied numbers 362 to 356 High Road. That included number 360 Chiswick High Road, where Richard Tyser first set up his business as Auctioneer and Estate Agent, in 1873.

At numbers 354 and 352, J. Walker & Company had their jewellery shop; then the boot makers, W. Abbott & Sons, before the showrooms of the Gas Light & Coke Company at numbers 348 and 346; followed by the tea rooms of J. Lyons & Company at numbers 344 and 342, with the next two numbers occupied by Montague Burton's tailor and outfitters shop, with a billiard hall occupying the upper floor.

Chiswick's one great drapers store was Goodbans Ltd. who occupied the adjacent premises and stretched from number 336 to number 326, with staff members provided with dormitory accommodation, if required by them, in rooms above the store.

Lilley & Skinner, the shoe and boot merchants, occupied numbers 324 and 322, with Mrs. A.H. Ward, fruiterer, next door, and MacFisheries occupying number 318; then Williamsons the confectioner, and Westminster Bank occupying the site on the corner of Clifton Gardens, along the flank of which was the entrance to Finnis, Downey & Company, the solicitors who occupied the first floor above the bank. A little way along Clifton Gardens was a three storey house occupied by Mr. & Mrs. Duer, who utilised some of the rooms in the house for short term lodgers, many of them show business personnel who were appearing at the nearby Chiswick Empire Theatre, some of whom became very well known, including Morcambe & Wise.

On the other corner of Clifton Gardens is Lloyds Bank, and at number 308 was the outfitters,Meakers Ltd., with one of W.H. Cullen's grocery shops next door, then F.W. Cheek, beer retailer, and the tobacconist, Albert Baker & Company at number 302; next door to which, on the corner of Holly Road, was situated the caterers known as "A.B.C." (the Aerated Bread Company).

Holly Road, like Clifton Gardens, ran north from Chiswick High Road to Chiswick Common Road, with the original General Post Sorting Office situated, in those days, on that corner of Clifton Gardens, a fact which explains why quite a large area of South Acton shares the postal code of "W4" with Chiswick.

In Holly Road, a short distance from the High Road, existed the premises occupied by the Poor Dispensary for Sick Animals. The other corner of Holly Road, number 298 Chiswick High Road, is occupied by Fred. Bateman & Company, the opticians, and next door was J. Lovibond & Sons, wine merchants, at number 292. L.E. Jolly Ltd., the cooked provisions merchants, occupied number 290, next to which was Calvert & Company, milliners and fancy goods, followed by the shop occupied by the United Dairies Ltd.; then W. & G. Forth, the fruiterers, at number 284, with Boots the Chemist on the corner of Fishers Lane, which was a narrow turning running north across Chiswick Common Road and under the embankment of the "Underground" Railway Lines that had sliced off the northern part of the original Turnham Green.

Set back from Fishers Lane, not far from the High Road, was the Primitive Methodist Church, which became the victim of enemy bombing during the Second World War.

On the other corner of Fishers Lane was the pawnbrokers, George & Company, with the bakers, C. Hollowood, next door, and at number 276 the Truform Boot Company had their shop, followed by grocers with the unusual name of "The World's Stores"; and then another shop occupied by W. & G. Forth, trading as cheese mongers.

R.C. Hammet Ltd. occupied number 270, at butchers, with Richards (hosiers) next door; then the Dolcis Shoe Company occupied numbers 266 and 264, and Rego Clothiers Ltd., the tailors were at numbers 262 and 260, with the Home & Colonial Stores between their shop and that of the Maypole Dairy Company at number 256.

Next came Dunn & Company, then known principally as hatters, followed by Rose Bros., boot dealers, and then at number 250, W. & G. Forth fruiterers, with Fips Ltd. (hosiers) next door, and on the corner of an alleyway which gave way to Bond Street, was the Fifty Shilling Tailors, gents outfitters. Bond Street was another turning between the High Road and Chiswick Common Road, which in those days, contained a few small, cottage type, houses let to tenants and owned by Mrs. Sheppard.

On the other side of Bond Street was the butchers shop of R.C. Hammett, then the provisions merchants, Lipton Ltd., followed by the "bazaar" of Marks & Spencer, at numbers 238 and 236, with the public house named "The Emperor" at numbers 234 and 232, and A.J. Fowkes had his estate agents office at number 230, followed by Bruces Ltd., chemists, then J. Maxwell, a tailor, and A.G. Rankin & Company at numbers 224 to 216, a drapery and carpet store stretching to the corner of Windmill Passage.

The public house named the "Windmill" is situated between Windmill Passage and the corner of Windmill Road, and in those days, the Standard Wallpaper Company had premises at the rear of the "Windmill", where they provided glass cut to customer's orders, also manufactured there some tiled surround fireplaces, which were much in vogue in the 1930's.

Some old, cottage style, houses still exist in that immediate area, including Castle Place, a short terrace off the end of Windmill Road, where it meets Chiswick Common Road, but those houses are now much altered and extended.

On the opposite corner of Windmill Road and the High Road, was the Chiswick Police Station, which had a small space for police cars in the yard behind, approached from Windmill Road, and next door to the Police Station, at number 208, was W. Davis, fruiterer; then Soutar & Company, grocers, followed by W.H. Smith's bookshop at number 204; with Churchills, the chemist, next door, then G.R. Newman, the fishmonger and poulterer, at number 200.

A.G. Hedges, the butcher, occupied the next shop, with another David Grieg shop at number 196, followed by H.G. Needham, the tobacconist, on the corner of Elliot Road, which also housed the office of "Robbie" Robinson, the editor of the "Brentford & Chiswick Times", above the shop.

On the other corner of Elliot Road, at number 192, was E.M. Hill, baker; then a draper G.H. White, followed by M. Bendel, confectioner, and Saunder Bros., grocery stores, and the provisions merchants, Cullens, had another shop at number 184, next door to Harris baby carriages, on the corner of Turnham Green Terrace.

The other corner of Turnham Green Terrace was known as "Ellis Corner" because the shop there was occupied by the wine merchants, Ellis & Company, and next door to them was Lilley & Skinner, the shoe merchants, at number 176, followed by William Mutton, (mantle warehouse); then A.B. Hemmings, the bakers, and A. Pearce, butcher, and at number 168, George Norrish had his ironmongery business. Next door again was another butcher, Adlington; then the dry cleaning business of Eastman & Son; with a tobacconist named "Amore" between them and William Cato & Sons, household stores at number 158, followed by the United Dairies shop, and S.W. Harrison, pharmacist; then Lockwood Bros., bakers; "Nuways" the dry-cleaners; and another David Grieg shop at number 148 on the corner of Mayfield Avenue.

Zeeta Co. Ltd. occupied the other corner at number 146, selling wonderful cakes and confectionery, and next door to them was the Express Dairy shop, followed by the tailors, Roberts & Barnett; then the Bush Radio Stores. At number 134 was Hammett, the butchers; then S. Budner's grocery shop, followed by the receiving office of the Royal Standard Laundry; next door to which was the provision merchants, Peark's Dairies. A popular butcher that specialised in savoury sausages, Rousham's, was at number 126, with Alexander & Sons, greengrocers, between the butcher and the public house named "The Roebuck" at number 122, on the corner of Thornton Avenue.

Beyond that terrace of shops there were more business premises, showrooms and shops including William Perrings furniture stores, also the tram depot and the Power House already referred to, and still further along some railway sidings for the delivery of coal, before the corner of Chiswick High Road and Goldhawk Road (known as "Young's Corner"), and the boundary of Hammersmith, was reached.

On the other side of Chiswick High Road, from the boundary with Hammersmith (British Grove) the buildings were principally residential, including Prebend Mansions (built on prebendary land), right up to Chiswick Lane, where the shopping area commenced on that southern side of the High Road. The corner shop, number 85, was occupied by H.C. Wheatland, electrical engineer, with Burley & Burley, watch makers, next door, followed by Jones Sewing Machine shop; then C. Dawes, confectioner, and at number 93, the Brentford & Chiswick Electricity Department showroom, with the restaurant of J. Perilli next door, on the corner of Cranbrook Road.

Spring Grove Laundry's receiving office was on the other corner of Cranbrook Road, followed by Walton's Fish Bar; then T. White, boot repairer, and Mrs. S. Stokes" restaurant at number 103, next door to the confectionery shop of Mrs. D. Douchkoff. Number 107 was occupied by N. Pearl, dyer and cleaner, with an upholsterer, D. Toper, next door; then estate agents, Redfern & Gimson, followed by F.L. Saville, furniture dealer, and Arundel Signs, with the Chiswick Stamp Shop at number 115; then the confectioner, K.M. McLean, and the dining rooms of A. Coulon and occupying numbers 121 and 123 were S. and J. Crompton, general dealers.

Next door to them was A.A. Edwards, stationer; then the funeral directors, W.S. Bond, followed by another Bush Radio Store; boot makers, R.H. Sparks & Son; then A.C. Bolton, furniture dealer, and occupying the site on the corner of Brackley Road, numbers 137 to 143, was the Blue & White Garage.

The public house, "Packhorse & Talbot" occupies the other corner and between it and the furniture dealer, M. Mallah, at number 149, was the entrance to Dr. G.E. French's house which was set back on a site running behind the Baptist Church in Annandale Road, and at number 153 Chiswick High Road, on the corner of Annandale Road, is still Barclays Bank.

From the Packhorse & Talbot the business development on that side of the High Road becomes gradually further back from the actual carriageway of the main road, and between it and the easterly entrance to Linden Gardens there is a separate pavement and carriageway, part of which was occupied, in those days, by an underground "Gents" toilet, and only a few years before 1936 that area was utilised by enterprising "entrepreneurs" as a market place, which market was very popular with the local public but not so popular with the local council authorities. Between the two entrances to Linden Gardens from the High Road, there still exists the footpath behind the shops in Chiswick High Road which crosses Duke Road into Bourne Place, and the footpath continues, from Dukes Avenue as Barley Mow Passage to Prospect Place.

Returning to the High Road at Annandale Road, on the western corner, at number 155, was the Chiswick Furniture Galleries, with the dining rooms of E. Simmons next door, then Victoria Wine Company, followed by J. Bowles & Sons, greengrocer, and T. Hurn, a butcher, with the pawnbroker, R. Hassell, at number 165, on the corner of Devonshire Road.

On the other corner was L. Blumenkehl, retailer of workmen's overalls and other clothing, next door to which was Len Green's gramophone shop (when he was joined by his brother the name of the shop became "Toogees", i.e. two Greens); then Mrs. D. Hawkins' cooked meats shop, followed by the leather merchant, E.H. Barnes, at number 173, with Mrs. A. Secombe, tobacconist, between his shop and the public house named "Prince of Wales". Next, at number 181, was Mrs. L. Bradbury, described as a wardrobe dealer; then Mrs. E. Lague's laundry, followed by another public house named "George the Fourth"; then Walley Hallett's dining rooms and the hairdresser, A. Goldsmith.

At number 191 there was an eel pie shop run by Mrs. E. Hutton, with F. Landgrebe, the popular baker next door, then an upholsterer, A. Imeson; grocer, George Curtis, and occupying numbers 197 and 199, was the Brentford & Chiswick Fire Brigade, with T.B. Gerard & Sons, the ironmongers, next door, followed by A. Murray, boot and shoe maker; then George Farquharson, a grocer, and G.H. Davis & Son, furniture dealer at number 207, with the site on the corner of the eastern entrance to Linden Gardens occupied by the "Chiswick New Market", the covered market place created by the local authority to eliminate the previous street market, already mentioned.

A.E. Thresher, the optician, occupied the other corner, with the florist, Mrs. G. Tatler, next door; then J & M Stone, radio engineers, followed at numbers 219 and 221, by the shoe shop of W.H. Dadds & Son, with another shop of J & M Stone on the other side at numbers 223 and 225, up to the corner of the western entrance to Linden Gardens.

On the opposite corner was the Standard Wallpaper Company, occupying numbers 227 and 229; then a parade of four shops, which in 1936 was a new development on the site up to the corner of Duke Road, previously occupied by an early cinema, number 229b being occupied by Miss M. Townend as a cafe; number 229c by N. Finley as a tobacconist and the corner shop, 229d, was occupied as a costumers by Warbrook Ltd..

On the other corner of Duke Road, numbers 231 to 235 High Road, was the outfitters, Noel Bros., and next to them was the ladies gowns shop with the name of "Margaret"; then the premises of the Times Furnishing Company occupying numbers 241 to 247 up to the corner of Dukes Avenue, with the Roman Catholic Church, "Our Lady of Grace" on the other corner and the Presbytery beside it.

Number 251 was occupied by Stewart Bros., house furnishers, and next door was the Express Dyers and Cleaners, followed by Edgar Elvin, the florist, with E.A. Johnson, ladies hairdresser adjoining.

A narrow passageway led through to Barley Mow Passage and

Strand-on-the-Green at the beginning of the century

Strand-on-the-Green during the 1930's

Office front for Centenary celebrations 1973

1987 October hurricane damage

on the other corner was the Chiswick Main Post Office occupying numbers 257 and 259 Chiswick High Road; then confectioners with the name of "The Bonanza"; and then Owen Hopkins, the optician, followed by F.W. Shears, the tobacconist; H.J. Edmunds, masseur; Mrs. Segal's circulating library, and on the corner, at number 269, was the watch merchants "Chancers". There was another passageway to Barley Mow Passage, then the Barley Mow Public House, continuing the bend of the High Road into Heathfield Terrace, with the two brothers occupying the remaining premises before Turnham Green Common, numbers 273 and 275 occupied by Captain Whitman trading as the estate agents "Whitman & Whitman", and his brother Colonel Whitman trading as H.J. Whitman & Sons, builders at numbers 277 and 279. Quite naturally that corner was referred to as "Whitman's Corner" and due to the wide stretch of carriageway at that junction, it was used by sundry motor coach companies as a collecting and dropping off point.

Situated close to that junction of Chiswick High Road with Heathfield Terrace, on Turnham Green Common, is the War Memorial obelisk, and the Common occupies the next stretch of the High Road up to Sutton Lane, broken by the Town Hall Avenue which leads directly down to the Chiswick Town Hall from the High Road and provided vehicle access to the Christ Church built on Turnham Green and consecrated in 1853 as Chiswick's second parish church.

On the north-west corner of Turnham Green, at the junction with Sutton Lane, there existed in 1936, one of Britain's first world war tanks, raised on a rock embankment, as a memorial.

On the other corner of Sutton Lane, at number 281 Chiswick High Road, is situated the Midland Bank, which had next door, in 1936, the United Dairies shop, followed by the confectionery shop of Miss M. Baldwin; then G. Beaton, the dentist, and R.J. Powlesland, the newsagent.

At number 293, F. Hawkins & Company traded as grocers, with the chemists, Timothy White & Taylor next door; then L. Zomerplaag, fruiterer, followed by C.F. Freeman, the butcher, at number 299; then J.H. Dent (oil and colour man) and at number 303, the Chiswick Electric Shop and Gatward Taylor & Company, signwriters. Number 305 was occupied by C. Loder, trading as a confectioner, with the dining rooms of W.J. Saw next door to him, on the corner of West Place, with Mrs. M. Weeks tobacconist shop on the other corner, followed by S. Miller, florist; then C. & S. Susman, boot repairers, and "Peggy's" Beauty Parlour (ladies hairdresser) next, with J.N. Hewett & Company, ironmonger, at number 315.

The dry cleaner, F.A. Read, was at number 317, next to which was the local butchers, Chubb & Dowden, followed by Jones & Company, boot and shoe merchants, and J.W. Ritchie, furniture dealer; then E.S. Motors, and on the corner of King's Place, at number 327, was the "Wine Celler". On the other corner of King's Place was Lusby's Bakery, with Broad & Company, printers, occupying numbers 331 and 333.

Next to the printers, at number 335, was, and still is, the timber merchants, G.R. Mumford & Company, beyond which, on that side of the High Road, the properties became mainly residential, with a petrol station – garage on one corner of Marlborough Road, and the private school, named "Oxford College", on the other corner.

In order to return to the offices of Messrs. Tyser, Greenwood & Company, one has to cross over to the northern side where, on the corner of Chiswick Road, at numbers 492 to 496 Chiswick High Road, Makin & Harrison traded as motor agents, with E.J.H. Clarke & Company, chartered accountants, in offices above, and next door was A.E. Gordon's cycle shop; then the Chiswick Tyre House, followed by Mrs. R. Levene's hairdressing salon, and at number 482, F. Read's valet service shop.

Another tobacconist, F. Battalion, was at number 480; then Rose Direct Milk Supplies, and at number 476, Miss J.E. Bigg was a certified midwife, and Miss F. Austin traded as a dressmaker. J. Jarvis traded as a greengrocer at number 474; then came Mrs. H. Mitchell's ladies outfitters, next to Line & Armstrong, printers, with C.F. Mutch, ham and beef dealer at number 466, followed by P.R. Graham, another ladies outfitters, then Miss L. Dunn, confectioner, and at number 460, Galloways Toy Shop.

Next came the Chiswick Hardware & Wallpaper Stores; then hairdresser C.T. Parks, followed by C. Bernard, gramophone and music dealer, and the restaurant of Y. Angelo. At number 450 was the public house named "Robin Hood" and next door was Henry Lawes, the gents outfitters; then the Hygenic Bakeries, and at number 444, Baldwin & Company, the house agents, followed by Gapp's grocery stores, and on the corner of Acton Lane, Mapograph Company, the school outfitters.

On the other corner of Acton Lane is the public house which has occupied that site for many generations, named "The Old Packhorse", behind which, in Acton Lane was a short terrace of small shops with the name of "Chiswick Terrace", the freehold of which had been acquired by Sir Oswald Stoll who erected a number of Palaces of Variety, each named "Empire" and the one at Chiswick was therefore the Chiswick Empire (others were at Shepherds Bush, Hackney, etc.), but between The Old Packhorse and the Chiswick Empire Theatre, were the undertakers, W.G. Barratt at number 430, and on the corner of the open space that surrounded the "Empire", was the stationers, Blissley & Company with three very small shops behind, facing the flank of the "Empire", number 426a being occupied by Fred. Coles, gents hairdresser; 426b by O. Wrigley's "Square Deal" sports outfitters, and 426c by the "Theatre Snack Bar".

Facing the other flank of the Chiswick Empire Theatre were four more very small shops, number 406a occupied by A.T.

Stainer, bootrepairer; 406b by Mrs. K. Huntley, confectioner, 406c by the receiving office of the Royal Standard Laundry, and 406d by the Cafe run by C. Green.

The corner shops, numbers 406 and 404, were occupied by William Cato & Sons, the hardware and household stores, next to which was the red brick building numbered 402 known as the "Smoker's Market", followed by E. Stevens & Company, confectioners, and the small house agents office of Green & Lines.

Set back from the pavement, behind a paved forecourt, was the old shop of R. Caught, the butcher who, at one time, had the animals delivered to him "on the hoof", i.e. alive, and they were collected on the forecourt and driven into his own abattoir beside and behind his shop. For many years, cricket has been played on that part of Turnham Green almost immediately across the High Road from his shop, and it became his practice to present a leg of lamb of any cricketer who managed to bat the cricket ball from one of the wickets into his forecourt.

Next came the newsagent's shop, Gardiner Bros., then a small shop run by George Cross as a gents outfitters, followed by E. Steven & Company, confectioners, and C. Hollowood's bakers shop at number 390.

The shop that was at number 388 was Usher's wines and spirits off licence, which very conveniently opened during the evenings, having closed during much of the normal daytime shopping hours, and the fact was a great convenience to the staff of Messrs. Tyser, Greenwood & Company at number 386, as keys to empty premises which interested purchasers wished to inspect outside normal office hours, could be left with the off licence for those people to collect in the evening.

As has already been mentioned, number 386 Chiswick High Road is on the corner of Essex Place Square and has an interesting front and return frontage window at the ground floor level, formed of moulded oak framing incorporating various shapes, into which bevel-edged, quarter plate glass is fitted, and a pair of front doors, to match, set back to form a porch. The entire front section of the two floored building is occupied by that firm of Surveyors, Auctioneers and Estate Agents, and the whole of the ground floor, at that time, stretching right back to Essex Place, the end section having been a stable, with cobble stoned floor and hay loft. The rear section of the upper floor, with an entrance along the flank of the building, was leased to Mr. N. Ramsay Murray, a much respected solicitor.

CHAPTER FIVE

"Wartime Chiswick"

THE imposition of "black-out" commenced as soon as the Second World War was declared in Britain at 11 a.m. on Sunday, 3rd September 1939, and the effect was to present difficulties to the average person used to travelling about the streets with reasonable lighting now totally eliminated and with vehicles moving about with very little lighting to show their presence. To assist the members of the public, some street curbs, also the trees lining the roads, were painted with bands of white paint, and for many years after the end of the war, in 1945, those white bands around the trees could be detected.

All young men were required to register for military service, including the author who, for reasons never explained, was not actually called upon until March of 1940. This was quite fortunate because the winter of 1939-1940 was very severe with the inevitable freezing of water supplies in some houses and other premises, and in some cases of very poorly maintained or neglected properties, roofs collapsed and the occupiers had to be found alternative homes. Houses that had been boarded up ready for demolition, being on the route of the proposed Great West Road Extension, were investigated and if reasonably possible, the services were reconnected and other work carried out to provide at least a temporary home for those people.

On the European continent the German troops having over-run Poland and entered a pact with Russia, turned their attention to France and the Low Countries and during the months of early summer in 1940, made tremendous advances by using their superior air power and modern methods of warfare, which prompted Italy to decide to join the war on the side of Germany on 10th June. Possibly that was a deciding factor, but in any event, the French Government asked for armistice and the British Forces had to evacuate the Continent with all possible haste.

As the likelihood of bombing became more acute, the Strand-on-the-Green School was evacuated to Cornwall.

Nazi Germany's next task was to eliminate the British air forces but in that they were not successful due to radar, two fighter aircrafts, the Hurricane and the Spitfire, and a host of brave young men, not only from the British Isles but also from around the British Empire, the United States of America, Europe including Poland.

Initially the German attacks were concentrated on airfields and manufacturing properties, but inevitably some bombs fell on London despite the capital having been ringed with hundreds of barrage balloons and anti-aircraft guns which were stationed in sundry open parklands and other suitable places.

The German airforce suffered losses during their daylight raids and the expected bombing of the London area did not commence until the autumn months and the bombing which did occur took place mainly during the hours of darkness.

Chiswick's first experience of bombing occurred on 4th September 1940, when a parachute flare was dropped over the Wellesley Road area, but the first high explosive bombs fell on the following day at the junction of the High Road with Netheravon Road, near the "Coach & Horses" resulting in Chiswick's first casualty, fortunately not fatal. Another parachute flare was dropped over the "Blue & White" garage on the corner of the High Road with Brackley Road, on 6th September, and that was followed two days later by a string of incendiary bombs over the Chiswick House Grounds, also 4 Hogarth Avenue and the Chiswick Cemetery; Corney Road; Burlington Lane and Chiswick Mall area.

On 10th September, high explosive bombs were dropped around Fishers Lane; Holly Road; Linden Gardens; Glebe Street; 44 Quick Road (which was destroyed); Hogarth Laundry; St. Joseph's Hospital; Chiswick Cemetery in Corney Road; L.E.P. Transport and the Promenade Approach Road, with another explosive bomb in the Bedford Park Area, at the South Parade end of Rusthall Avenue.

The air-raids must have persisted on the following nights for although no further bombs were reported in the Chiswick area, there were a number of reports of Anti-Aircraft shells falling over a wide area from Brentford, over the Great West Road, at 30 Grosvenor Road; 4 Beverley Road; L.E.P. at Church Wharf; 6 Hogarth Lane; St. John's School in Brook Road; on the Southern Railway line; and on the London Passenger Transport Board's Sports Grounds in Bollo Lane.

The next high explosives were dropped on 14th September, one on that side of Harvard Road, which had been earmarked for the Great West Road Extension, opposite to Churchdale Court, and another on Grove Park Road and Riverview Road.

There were some more Anti-Aircraft shells dropped on 15th September, and surprisingly machine gun bullets at 21 Annandale Road and in Elliott Road.

Shortly afterwards it was discovered that damage had occurred to houses in Chiswick, 2 Hadley Gardens and numbers 41 to 51 Windmill Road, from trailing barrage balloon cables.

An unexploded bomb landed on the south-west side of the Central School which subsequently exploded damaging the School and 48 and 50 Staveley Road, on the 17th September, also two other high explosive bombs landed behind numbers 93 to 97 Park Road.

On the following evening high explosive bombs fell on 9 Blenheim Road; 3 Newton Grove; 13 Blandford Road; on Southfield and Hawkshead Roads in the Bedford Park area, and an incendiary bomb landed in Kings Place, near 329 Chiswick High Road.

There were two high explosive bombs on 20th September, which landed on gravel pits near Chiswick Bridge and the railway line, but the biggest incident which had occurred so far was on 21st September when a parachute mine exploded over the recreation ground at the rear of Thames Road, in the Strand-on-the-Green area, causing extensive damage to property in that neighbourhood. The author whose training at the Royal Artillery School of Survey, on Salisbury Plain, had ended just when the Dunkirk evacuation of British troops occurred resulting in a long delay before he was posted to the Third Survey Regiment, R.A., eventually managed to obtain leave to visit his hometown, including a visit to a cottage in Thames Road, the home of a friend, which had been very seriously damaged by that mine, found the building almost non-existent, yet sitting intact on a mantel shelf of a fireplace, was a delicate, glass covered, decorative ornament. Also on that day, in the Bedford Park area, anti-aircraft shells exploded near 19 Blandford Road and 40 Southfield Road.

It was the Brentford area that suffered from high explosive bombs on 24th September, the places affected being the Brentford Docks; the Gas Light & Coke Company's premises at Montgomery Wharf; St. Paul's Road and Back Lane; the Half Acre; Clifden Road and the railway line near Brentford Station. Chiswick had a number of incendiary bombs including one which burnt out the Gunnersbury Baptist's Manse in Burlington Road, and another which badly damaged 2 Reckitt Road.

More high explosive bombs fell the following night affecting the Clayponds Isolation Hospital; properties in Lionel Road; Gunnersbury Park; Brentford Market; Ernest Gardens and

Magnolia Road, also a parachute mine demolished eight houses in Ellesmere Road, with one person killed and ten others injured. In addition, more high explosive bombs fell in Chiswick Lane; Upham Park Road; Ennismore Avenue; the old Tram Depot; Flanders Mansions and Road; Prebend Gardens and South Side.

The Borough was at the receiving end of more high explosive bombs on 26th September affecting properties in Braemar Road; Latewood Road; Brook Lane and Road; the premises of R. & J. Parks off Thames Road and the railway bridge across Thames Road; 5 Strand-on-the-Green; Grove Park Road and Terrace and both 24 and 60 Hartington Road.

The Piccadilly Railway Line near Boston Manor Station received a high explosive bomb on the night of 27th September, and a number of incendiary bombs affected the Bus Garage in Belmont Road and Essex Place, also the Army & Navy Stores in Heathfield Terrace, as well as a string of others throughout the Chiswick area.

The following night more high explosive bombs affected properties in Cornwall Grove; Eastbury Grove; Pages Yard; Church Wharf and Hogarth Lane, also the Hudson Essex premises in the Great West Road; Gunnersbury Avenue; Chiswick High Road; 2 Oxford Road and the railway line near Gunnersbury Station; 36 Wellesley Road; 46 Barrowgate Road; 60 Sutton Court Road; 8 Milnthorpe Road and the Chiswick House Grounds, also the recreation grounds in Southfield Road.

There was no let up of this torment which continued the next evening with more high explosive bombs affecting 44 Elliott Road; 48 Thornton Avenue, the old Tram Depot; Grove Park Road; Kinnaird Avenue; Bolton Road; the stadium at the Polytechnic Sports Grounds; Cubitts Yacht Basin; the Great Chertsey Road, also at Brentford, Boston Manor Park;30 Swyncombe Avenue; the London Playing Fields; 30 Brook Road South; 27 Mafeking Avenue and the Metropolitan Water Board's premises in Kew Bridge Road, and two further bombs on 160 Rusthall Avenue and 4 Vanburgh Road in Bedford Park. In addition, there were a number of incendiary bombs scattered throughout both Brentford and Chiswick that night, including one on the Bedford Park Club premises in The Avenue.

More high explosive bombs were dropped on 30th September, on 221 Popes Lane and Gunnersbury Park (where Anti-Aircraft guns were deployed), also in Mulliner's Works off Bath Road; 74 Chiswick High Road; 33 Chiswick Lane; St. Joseph's Hospital again; Corney Road; Edensor and Grantham Roads, and the Promenade Approach Road.

The first day of October brought more bombing with high explosives affecting Sutton Court Road and Cedars Road in Chiswick, and Boston Gardens and Park in Brentford. Apart from a number of incendiary bombs dropped around the Chiswick area during the next night, there was no serious bombing until 4th October when high explosive bombs fell on Henley's premises on the Great West Road, also in Gunnersbury Park where more bombs fell the next evening, also another on the Ibis Sports Grounds near Hartington Road; and on the 6th October some incendiary bombs fell on the Chiswick Products Works and in the High Street in Brentford.

On 8th October an unexploded bomb was found at Manor Court, just off Gunnersbury Avenue, and other bombs exploded in the nearby 24 Princes Avenue and in Gunnersbury Park yet again; also at 88 Duke Road; 43 and 45 Reckitt Road; at the rear of 39 and 41 Wolseley Gardens, and there was also a number of incendiary bombs throughout the Gunnersbury area.

There was a quiet night locally on 9th October and the only incident on 10th October was a high explosive bomb in Oxford Road.

That brief lull continued until 13th October when more high explosive bombs fell locally on 41 and 43 Burlington Lane; at the back of Eyot House on Chiswick Mall; on Homefields Recreation Grounds; 25 Homefield Road; 24 Chiswick Lane; in the middle of Turnham Green Terrace and at 1 Flanders Road; also a number of incendiary bombs scattered throughout the Chiswick area.

On the 14th October a high explosive bomb fell on Edwards Engineering Works on the Great West Road and in Brentford's Kenley and Pottery Roads; the High Street and North Road, also on the railway line beside Green Dragon Lane.

More high explosive bombs fell on 15th October affecting Elmwood Road; 21 Fauconberg Road; Whitehall Park Road; Thames Road; Oxford Road; 40 Grange Road; in the grounds of the Catholic Grammar School; and a barge on the river beside the Gas Light & Coke Company's Works at Brentford.

Gunnersbury Avenue and Lane received more high explosives on 16th October, with just one high explosive the next night on 47 Netheravon Road, plus incendiary bombs on Mawson Lane; Chiswick Lane and Airedale Avenue.

Brentford received the high explosives on 18th October, at 58 Clayponds Avenue; Crowther Avenue; Brentwick Gardens and Carville Park North, whilst Chiswick had a number of incendiary bombs affecting the Gunnersbury area.

Just one incident occurred on 19th October, and that was a high explosive bomb which landed on the railway line near Chiswick Southern Railway Station, but more high explosives fell on 20th October on Power Road; the London Passenger Transport Works; on the Great West Road near the Duke of York public house; at 1 to 4 Apple Garth; also on 15 and 18 Devonshire Gardens; in Turnham Green Terrace near the railway station; 2 Mayfield Avenue, and on St. Catherine's Court in Bedford Park, plus an incendiary bomb at 15 Queen Anne's Gardens.

Two high explosive bombs fell on 21st October in Chiswick House Grounds and on the Kensington Cemetery off the Great

West Road, which was followed by a short respite locally until 24th when two unexploded bombs fell in Lionel Road.

On the 25th October, however, a number of high explosives fell affecting 3 Challis Road; 33 St. Mary's Grove; 33, 56, and 64 Burnaby Gardens; 98 Grove Park Road; St. Thomas's Sports Grounds; Sutton Court; Fauconberg Road; Chiswick House Grounds near the obelisk gate in Burlington Lane, plus a number of incendiary bombs; whilst Brentford received the high explosives the following night at Holly House, Boston Manor Road; Somerset Road and in the High Street.

On the 28th October, high explosives fell on the London Passenger Transport Works; in Silver Crescent and in Thorneyhedge Road. There occurred another brief respite until 3rd November when high explosive bombs fell on 77 and 79 Prebend Gardens.

On the 4th November 1940, high explosive bombs fell in the middle of the Great West Road; on 48 Adelaide Terrace; on Alvis Works in Brook Lane North; on 30 Layton Road and along the railway line, also on Dorey's Yard in Brook Lane North.

Strangely there was no bombing affecting the Borough on 5th November, but during the following evening high explosives fell on The Ridgeway; Princes Avenue; the London Passenger Transport Works on the railway line, and on the foreshore between Barnes Railway Bridge and the Civil Service Boat House.

More high explosives fell on 7th November, this time again on the Kensington Cemetery; on the railway line between Gunnersbury Avenue and the Great West Road; on the Hudson Essex Works and the Great West Road; 487 Chiswick High Road; 16 Cambridge Road; Oxford Road; Edensor Road; the Chiswick County School; on allotments near the Memorial Homes; on Spencer Road; the Polytechnic Sports Grounds and 24 Hartington Road.

There was another short respite until 10th November, when

high explosives fell on the foreshore near Goats Wharf and Ferry lane in Brentford; Town Meadow Depot; the Gas Light & Coke Company's works at Magnolia Wharf; the Brentford Docks; Brentford Soap Works, Catherine Wheel Road; 117 and 118 High Street; the Boar's Head public house yard; Chiswick Products Sports Grounds; 58 Elmwood Road; St. Michael's Vicarage on the corner of Elmwood Road with Sutton lane; 48 Sutton Court Road (immediately opposite to the Methodist Church); Gunnersbury Preparatory School; 22 Burnaby Gardens; 44 St. Mary's Grove; the West London Timber Yard; 71 Riverview Grove; Thames Road; 10 Grove Park Terrace and 68 Grove Park Road. On the night of 12th November, a high explosive bomb fell within the grounds of the Catholic Grammar School at Gunnersbury.

The next bombing experienced locally was on 16th November when high explosives fell into the St. James Church Yard in the Chiswick High Road, and another onto 461 to 465 Chiswick High Road; the Gardiner's Arms on the corner of Surrey Crescent; onto 4 Clarence Road; in Stonehill Road; on 81, 140 and 142 Wellesley Road, also the Plough Inn public house in Kew Bridge Road. Others fell in the Chiswick High Road opposite to Woolworth's Store and four fell in Boston Manor Park, as well as a number of incendiary bombs across Chiswick, mainly south of the High Road. One night passed without bombs locally but on 18th November a number of high explosives fell in Boston Manor Road and Boston Manor Park, including one into the lake.

There followed a much appreciated break from bombing locally and it was eleven days before the next which occurred on 29th November when a high explosive landed on 16 Manor Gardens and others on the Sports Grounds of the London Passenger Transport Board; on 1 Belmont Grove; Watchfield Court in Sutton Court Road; 1 Sharon Road; 26 Alwyn Avenue; 22 and 24 Wavendon Avenue; 3 Eastbourne Road, also in Chesterfield, Chatsworth and Lawfords Roads, also on 24 Hartington Road;

Cubitts Yacht Basin; in Grove Park Terrace; Fauconberg Road; St. Thomas's Sports Grounds; 23 to 27 Grove Park Gardens; 4 Grove Park Road; 20 and 22 Hartington Road; Fullers Brewery in Chiswick Lane, and others in Netheravon Road; Chiswick Lane and Chiswick Mall, also on the foreshore of Chiswick Mall, opposite to Chiswick Lane.

More high explosives fell that night, one close to the Gas Light & Coke Company's works at Brentford, and in the Bedford Park area in The Avenue by Speldhurst Road; on 54 Fielding Avenue; 2 Brookfield Road; on the corner of Fielding Road and Queen Anne's Gardens; 81 Whellock Road and at the rear of 87 Spelhurst Road. In addition there was a number of incendiary bombs over a wide area of Brentford.

On the next night more high explosives fell but this time confined to Hartington Court in Hartington Road.

December 1940 started with a week of quietness without local bombing, but on the 8th a number of high explosives fell in the Brentford area affecting Clayponds Avenue; Carville Crescent; Brentwick Gardens; Lionel Road and several in Gunnersbury Park. That was followed by another lull in local bombing until 22nd December, when a high explosive bomb fell in Thames Road.

Christmas 1940 and the early New Year of 1941 were thankfully free from local bombing, but on 10th January high explosives fell on the Polytechnic Sports Grounds and the Ibis Boathouse grounds, also on the nearby bank of the River Thames.

Incendiary bombs fell in the area north and south of Chiswick High Road at the Hammersmith end, on 16th January 1941, but no high explosives until 19th January when one fell on the south side of the Great West Road by the canal bridge. No local bombing was experienced until the last day of January when high explosives fell on the Open Air Swimming Baths in Edensor Road, and on allotments near the L.E.P. Transport Depot near Corney Road.

Mercifully there was no bombing throughout the whole of

February in the Chiswick area, and the only bombing during March involved incendiary bombs around the whole of the local area and an exploding anti-aircraft shell on the tennis courts in Chiswick House Grounds.

April 1941 was also fairly quiet apart from some high explosives in the Brentford Park area which demolished 68 to 74 Greenend Road, with some bombs falling on the railway lines at the rear, and a couple of unexploded anti-aircraft shells, one at Hartington Court and the other in Brentford.

During May of 1941 there were a few incidents including both high explosives and incendiary bombs falling on the Chiswick Products Bowling Green.

A new "Type G Mine" was exploded on 7th June over Princes Avenue, off Gunnersbury Avenue, damaging at least two hundred houses, also some high explosive bombs fell on the London Passenger Transport Works.

That proved to be the last of the bombing experienced locally not only for the rest of 1941, but also for the whole of 1942, and although no bombs fell locally during 1943, air raids must have continued because some anti-aircraft shells fell and exploded on 18th January, on Wilkinson's Sword Factory and at 18 Alexandra Road, also 1 St. Albans Avenue on 22nd January. Again on 3rd March more anti-aircraft shells landed at 16 Oxford Road; at St. Georges Church, and in the centre of the railway track opposite to the Old Kew Signal Box.

Later in that year, on 7th October 1943, an unexploded anti-aircraft shell fell on the Riverside Lawn Tennis Club in Burlington Lane.

Increased bombing activity arrived in January 1944 and a high explosive bomb fell on the 5th along the promenade approach Road and on the Promenade itself, with more anti-aircraft shells exploding on 21st at 10 Spencer Road and in Boston Manor Road, also another on 29th in the Kensington Cemetery.

That was followed on 19th February with a high explosive bomb on the corner of the High Road and Dukes Avenue, damaging the Roman Catholic Church and nine shops, also another on the Red Arrow Garage, and that bombing closed the Chiswick High Road to traffic for a week.

More bombing occurred on 20th February, firstly with an unexploded high explosive in Gunnersbury Park together with another that did explode, also more high explosives in Cavendish Road and Spencer Road, where two houses were demolished, and on the Polytechnic Sports Grounds and on the Convent in Chiswick Lane. In addition, there were three unexploded bombs at 35 Chiswick Lane; on Mayfield Garage and incendiary bombs in Staveley Road and other places throughout Chiswick including Turnham Green Terrace and 10 South Parade.

More high explosives fell on 23rd February 1944 on 4 and 22 Bolton Road; 23 Spencer Road; 29 to 33 Wolseley Gardens; at the United Dairies premises in Sutton Lane; on 44 and 46 Barrowgate Road; 71 Ellesmere Road; 13 Milnthorpe Road; 30 Park Road; six in Chiswick House Grounds together with four unexploded bombs. There was also a number of incendiary bombs throughout the Chiswick area, plus two anti-aircraft shells on Watchfield Court in Sutton Court Road.

On 24th February more high explosives fell on the allotments near Boston Manor Station and on the Playing Fields in Boston Gardens, also at 163 High Street, Brentford; on Kew Bridge Station; Stile Hall Mansions; in the centre of St. Alban's Avenue; at the rear of 72 Speldhurst Road, together with several incendiaries and more in Chiswick House Grounds and at 109 Park Road. In addition, a parachute bomb exploded over playing fields behind the Congregation Church in Boston Manor Road.

Apart from some incendiary bombs around the Brentford and Boston Manor area during March, there occurred another short respite from air-raids affecting the local area. However, scientists in Germany had been working on an unmanned, rocket propelled flying machine which was fitted with explosives designed to ignite upon impact. These flying bombs were named "Victory One" (V1) by the inventors, and "Doodle-bugs" by the Londoners who started to experience those infernal machines in June of 1944. They were launched from various places on the near Continent and flew in a straight line until the rocket fuel was used up and then they just dropped to the ground where they exploded. The new weapon proved unnerving to the population in the first instance, and the British defence methods had to be reorganised.

It proved difficult to locate the individual launchings and to deploy fighter aircraft to shoot them down over the English Channel, but by moving a large proportion of the anti-aircraft artillery units to the Isle of Wight and along the south coast of England, it became possible to shoot down many of the V1s before they reached London.

Never-the-less, on 18th June 1944, one of those V1s dropped on Cubitts Yacht Basin, and on 24th June another in the grounds of the Chiswick Grammar School and houses in Staveley Gardens were damaged. On 26th June another dropped in Southfields Road near the junction with Rugby Road; and again on 30th June, three houses were destroyed, 69 severely damaged and 17 partially damaged when a V1 dropped onto Thornton and Mayfield Avenues.

The next V1 that dropped locally was on 6th July, this time on the Homefields and Chiswick Lane area, resulting in 16 houses being partially demolished; 66 seriously damaged and 608 slightly damaged, illustrating the widespread devastating effect of those infernal machines.

Despite all the defensive endeavours, the V1 continued to fall locally, one on 12th July destroyed four houses; seriously damaged seventeen others; partially destroyed eight others and damaged a total of 362 other houses in Brentford when it landed at 63

Clayponds Avenue, whilst another V1 which fell on Ferry Lane on 17th July 1944, extensively damaged the Gas Light & Coke Company's premises and a Great Western Railway Depot, also seriously damaged thirteen houses and less seriously damaging 359 other houses.

On 21st July, another V1 fell on Apple Garth, Chestnut Avenue, Brentford, damaging to a greater or lesser extent, a total of 775 dwellings, whilst our neighbours in Hammersmith received another V1 on 24th July, which did extensive damage there, but also damaged numbers 2 to 14 Chiswick High Road.

They continued to arrive throughout August of 1944, one on the 3rd fell on 23 Hartington Road; another on 20th fell on the playing fields of Chiswick Grammar School, damaging nearby almshouses and three houses in Grantham Road. Yet another fell on 21st which landed in the grounds of the Central School damaging not only the school but also houses in Burlington Lane; Staveley Road and Park Road, and even damaged some houses in Wilmington Avenue; and a second V1 fell on the quadrangle of the Grammar School damaging the school building and a number of houses in Burlington Lane and Grantham Road, also the block of Council Flats known as Alexandra Mansions.

On 23rd August another V1 fell at the rear of the Chiswick Polytechnic School in Bath Road, partially destroying the college and severely damaging houses in both Flanders and Bath Roads.

The last V1 to fall locally was on the 29th August 1944, outside numbers 107 and 109 Boston Manor Road, both houses being destroyed and a number of others being seriously damaged.

On 6th June 1944 the Allied Forces invaded Normandy and having managed to establish a good bridgehead began making steady progress into France and the Low Countries. Possibly the advance of those Allied Forces resulted in all the launching sites of the V1s to be over-run, but the Londoners were pleased to know that the onslaught of those "Doodlebugs" had come to an end.

However, German rocket scientists had been working for quite a long time on another weapon of destruction which they had named "Victory 2", which was in the form of a very large rocket, the nose-cap of which was packed with high explosives designed to explode upon impact. The rocket was designed to reach up into the higher reaches of the atmosphere, on a calculated trajectory so that when the rocket fuel expired the rocket itself would fall, literally out of the sky, on to its target.

The target was intended to be London, and by a strange twist in fate, the very first successful launching of the V2 by the German Forces, caused it to land in Chiswick. It landed in September 1944, without any warning whatsoever, in the middle of the carriageway of Staveley Road, outside number 5, resulting in numbers 1 to 5 and 14 to 20 Staveley Road being destroyed, with fifteen other houses seriously damaged and 559 other houses being damaged to a lesser degree.

Not wishing to cause public alarm, and the rocket having landed in the middle of the road, the initial reports that there had been a serious gas explosion was allowed to circulate. In due course, with subsequent V2s, the true explanation leaked out, but the only other similar incident experienced locally was one which arrived on 21st March 1945, on Packard's premises in the Great West Road, spreading damage in Brentford as far away as Carville Crescent and also extensively damaging properties in Heston.

One of those Nazi German rocket scientists was Werner von Braun, who was captured during the advances of the Allied Forces on the Continent, and he was transported to the United States of America, with other colleagues, and they formed the team with American scientists at N.A.S.A. which enabled the Americans to send men to the moon, some years later. Werner von Braun wrote a book which he entitled – "I Aimed For the Moon" and it is reported that it prompted Jack Benny to remark – "I Aimed For the Moon – and Hit London".

The 8th May 1945 was greeted as "Victory in Europe Day" following the suicide of Adolph Hitler and the unconditional surrender of the German forces and, not long afterwards, on the 14th August the Japanese forces also surrendered following the dropping of atomic bombs on two of their cities. Hiroshima and Nagasaki.

It was in 1945 that a well known actor and film star, Michael Redgrave, who had married actress Rachel Kempson in 1935, purchased "Bedford House" on Chiswick Mall for occupation by his family and they remained there until the children became adult and were themselves involved in the world of entertainment, so in 1954 the house was sold back to Sir Arthur Ellis.

The end of hostilities in Europe enabled the Mayor and Corporation of the Borough of Brentford & Chiswick to involve themselves in matters of public concern and a programme was prepared with an address by the Mayor, Alderman T.W. Stroud, J.P., M.C.C. which read–

> "With the close of hostilities in Europe, our thoughts naturally turn to post-war reconstruction problems, among the most urgent of which is HOUSING. We must provide more and better homes, but in planning these dwellings, regard must be had, not only to construction, elevation and other architectural features, but also to those modern domestic appliances and improvements which assist in the smooth and easy running of the house. We must plan and build wisely with full regard to the future home as well as present needs, so posterity will not say of us that we pursued a short-sighted housing policy. The people must have houses, but let these be properly designed on well planned and developed estates of which we may be justly proud.
>
> Under present conditions, it is essential and wise that we should build emergency homes, but we must ensure these are

only tempory. The need for this type of dwelling must not detract from nor weaken our determination to provide permanent houses. Beauty and pleasant surroundings are powerful health-giving tonics, let these be cardinal features in our future homes. Our task is great, but with the help and encouragement of all Burgesses, I am sure we shall succeed".

Field Marshall Sir Bernard L. Montgomery, G.C.B., D.S.O., who had lived in Chiswick as a boy and who was married at St. Nicholas Church in Old Chiswick, was offered the Freedom of the Borough of Brentford & Chiswick by the Mayor and Corporation, which he was pleased to accept, so following the cessation of hostilities in Europe, arrangements were made for the presentation, and the event took place on Saturday, 28th July 1945.

Appreciating that the great number of people who would wish to be present at the actual handing over of the presentation, could not be accommodated within the Chiswick Town Hall, arrangements were made to hire the Chiswick Empire which was suitably positioned overlooking Turnham Green at the opposite end of Town Hall Avenue. At 2.30 p.m. the Field Marshall was met at the borough boundary in the Great West Road, by the Mayor, Alderman T.W. Stroud, J.P., M.C.C., and the Town Clerk, Mr. John Skinner, with a landau, in which open carriage they proceeded to Turnham Green where the Field Marshall inspected a Guard of Honour provided by the 30th Battalion the Middlesex Regiment, whilst the Band of the 2nd Battalion the Middlesex Regiment were playing.

The party then entered the Chiswick Empire where music was provided by the Band of His Majesty's Irish Guards, including a fanfare of trumpets to announce the arrival of the honoured guest. The Town Clerk read the resolution conferring the Honourary Freedom which read–

"At a special meeting of the Town Council of the Borough of Brentford & Chiswick held at the Town Hall, Chiswick, London, W.4. on Tuesday, the 24th day of July 1945, it was resolved unanimously that under and in pursuance of the powers conferred by section 259 (2) of the Local Government Act, 1933, Field Marshall Sir Bernard Law Montgomery, Knight Grand Cross of the Most Honourable Order of the Bath, Companion of the Distinguished Service Order, a former resident of Chiswick, be admitted to be an Honourary Freeman of the Borough of Brentford & Chiswick in recognition of distinguished services rendered to his King and Country".

The Mayor then presented the Field Marshall with the Scroll recording the Freedom, together with a Presentation Clock made by the Goldsmiths and Silversmiths Company, a reproduction Cromwellian clock, bearing an inscription which read–

Presented with the Honourary Freedom of the Borough of Brentford and Chiswick by the Corporation of Brentford and Chiswick to Field Marshall Sir Bernard Law Montgomery, G.C.B., D.S.O., a former resident of Chiswick, in recognition of distinguished services rendered to his King and Country.

The inscription concluded with the date, 28th July 1945, and was emblazoned with the Arms of Montgomery and of Brentford and Chiswick.

Monty (as he was known affectionately) then signed the Roll of Freemen and thanked the assembled crowds, and following the playing of the National Anthem, he accompanied the Mayor to the Town Hall for tea. The ceremony concluded with the Mayor and the Field Marshall travelling in the landau to the other borough boundary at Young's Corner.

The year of 1945 saw not only the end of World War Two, but also the first General Election in Great Britain since 1936, which resulted in a Labour Government being elected to Parliament with a large majority which led to considerable changes in many aspects of life in this Country.

CHAPTER SIX

"The Post War Years"

WAR TIME restrictions were necessarily continued after the end of hostilities and the rationing of food, clothes and several other commodities continued for several years. Couples getting married and setting up home found that essential items such as curtaining for windows and floor covering, were in such short supply that they could only be legally acquired with special coupons issued to such couples by the Government, and then only a very limited amount of either for the first year, with the remaining small amount during the following year. The same applied to furniture although it was possible to obtain second-hand furniture but at a very high price. The furniture made available to newly married couples was known as "Utility Furniture" which proved to be well made and substantial.

During the war years the manufacture of motor vehicles was extremely restricted and new cars were only available to those considered by the government to need one for their work, many forms of employment having been classified as "Reserved Occupations". The effect was that those in "Reserved Occupations" were able to buy a new car for their own use every year or so, selling off their former car at a figure far in excess of the price given by them for the new car a year or so before. As with furniture, the cost of buying a second hand car proved to be very high for the first few years after the end of the war.

Restrictions were also placed on building materials and building work of any magnitude, it being necessary for a special building licence to be obtained from government sources before any form of renovation or building work could be put in hand.

There was some resentment to those restrictions, particularly when it was discovered that no such restrictions seem to apply when the government wished to erect new office blocks for their own use, such as the enormous block of government offices on the border between Kensington and Hammersmith which was named "Charles House" to mark the occasion of the birth of Charles who became His Royal Highness, the Prince of Wales.

The need for residential housing had already been appreciated by the local authorities and a Government scheme was put in hand to create temporary housing accommodation by the erection of "prefabricated" dwellings on suitable sites such as those created by the clearance of bombed buildings, also along the fringes of common land. Chiswick had a number of those prefabricated houses erected in a number of places including Strand-on-the-Green area of Magnolia and Thames Roads, in Duke Road, and on the Back Common part of Turnham Green.

Following the destruction of the Church of St. Mary Magdalene in Bennett Street by bombing during the war, as well as many houses in that area known as "New Chiswick", the congregation had either joined the people in St. Nicholas Church, or gone to other churches and, in any event, the remaining houses in that area were due for demolition, so rather than rebuild the Church as previously, it was agreed, during 1946, that a new Hall and premises should be built on the site in Bennett Street, for the congregation of St. Nicholas Church.

The new Labour Government also put in hand their plans to nationalise several services such as road, and rail transport, and coal mines.

During 1948, therefore, the London Passenger Transport

ceased to be a private company when all such transport facilities were nationalised and their works at Gunnersbury became part of London Transport.

During 1951, Hogarth House, which had been saved from severe dilapidation by Col. R.W. Shipway, J.P. and handed over to the Middlesex County Council, had been sufficiently renovated for it to be opened to the public.

An area north of the High Road which included Holly Road, Clifton Gardens and Belmont Grove had been earmarked for redevelopment by the local authority, including a comparatively obscure row of small houses which had existed from the beginning of the eighteenth century, situated off Holly Road, behind "Goodban's Store", which was known originally as Jessop's Row, but later renamed Jessop's Road, and demolition commenced with that row of houses in 1951.

During those early years after the Second World War the author had returned to his studies in order to qualify as a Chartered Surveyor which became increasingly difficult due to a number of reasons, not the least of which was the whole deluge of new legislation being passed by Parliament, much of which fundamentally affected the property profession. Never-the-less he qualified as a Chartered Auctioneer & Estate Agent in 1953, and shortly afterwards as a Chartered Surveyor, being elected as a fellow of both Institutions in 1963 and 1964, respectively.

Returning to those years immediately following the end of the war, a need to have a motor vehicle was apparent to the author who had acquired a Morris 8 saloon car (second hand) during the early years of the war, but unfortunately when petrol rationing ceased for all but a chosen few, and the author was posted overseas, that car had been laid up in his father's garage at the bottom of the garden. Even more unfortunately the car was destroyed when incendiary bombs set fire to the garage and the compensation received from the War Damage Commission was limited to only twenty-five pounds. At least ten times that amount was necessary to acquire even a very small car during those years immediately after the end of the war, but the author managed to purchase an old Austin 7 saloon car and renovated it sufficiently to commence using it for business purposes. By co-incidence, George Bradley, the author's colleague in Messrs. Tyser, Greenwood & Company, had also realised that a car would be required for business purposes, and he happened to purchase a small Austin sports car at about the same time and both he and the author introduced that "revolutionary" idea to the partners of their firm.

War Damage restoration work involved quite a fair proportion of the professional work of Messrs. Tyser, Greenwood & Company for some years after the war, and Ernest Parsons became almost exclusively involved in that work which involved agreeing with the Government appointed surveyor, the extent of work required to each individual property, also the cost of carrying out that agreed work. Such involved contact with a number of builders and one with whom the firm dealt with quite extensively at that time was a Mr. Richard Ball who later extended his business locally and built houses and flats in the Chiswick area, even buying a vacant site in Barrowgate Road on which he built a splendid house for occupation by himself and his family.

For generations it had been accepted that the most economic method of heating was by means of open coal burning fires in individual rooms, certainly in homes, and frequently also in offices and business properties, although gas fires had become more popular as being less labour intensive. Certain public buildings were heated by means of water filled radiators, the water being heated from coal, coke, or anthracite burning, or sometimes gas fired, boilers, and since the beginning of the twentieth century, heating by means of electricity had become more readily available but was considered more expensive and more dangerous. Coal fires were still relatively inexpensive and were accordingly more popular, but the combustion of coal in open fires produce a considerable amount of smoke, which during the winter months added to the foggy conditions for which London, in particular, had become quite notorious. A particularly serious period of such black foggy conditions was experienced in the early 1950's, one period lasting several days, resulting in an alarming rise in the number of residents dying of respiratory difficulties. That brought about Government action to eliminate the use of coal in favour of "smokeless" fuel, and an Act of Parliament was passed in 1956, entitled the "Clean Air Act", whereby, under local authority jurisdiction, areas were declared "Clean Air Zones" following the adoption, with appropriate government grants, all the means of heating within that zone were amended to methods which eliminated the use of coal.

The internationally known Chiswick Products amalgamated during 1954, with Messrs.Reckitt & Colman.

Possibly the first, post war, appreciable new private residential development in Chiswick, was the building during 1956, on a section of land between Cubitts Yacht Basin and the end house in Hartington Road, which development became known as "Thames Village".

The Treaty of Rome was signed during March of 1957, by France, Germany, Belgium, the Netherlands, Luxembourg and Italy, whereby the European Economic Council was formed. The United Kingdom subsequently endeavoured to join the European Economic Council but was frustrated by the President de Gaulle of France. However, when Edward Heath became Prime Minister, he was able to take the United Kingdom into the E.E.C. during 1973.

The Second World War had delayed the proposed Great West Road Extension through Chiswick by some twenty years, but during 1957, the London County Council commenced the necessary work in their area, so the Ministry of Transport commenced appropriate works on the Chiswick section of the project, which unfortunately resulted in the demolition of the Little Sutton Alms Houses in Sutton Lane. It was in that same year of 1957 that the Brentford & Chiswick Local History Society was formed, just to late to enable representations being made against the demolition of those alms houses.

The next appreciable new residential development occurred following the acquisition by the Borough of Brentford & Chiswick from the St. Thomas's Hospital authorities, of their sports grounds which occupied the area of land on the south side of Fauconberg Road, stretching back to the railway line, and the west side of Sutton Court Road back to Grove Park Terrace. In order to retain the link with St. Thomas's Hospital, roads within the estate were given names such as St. Thomas's Road and Nightingale Close, with a central section being retained for an infants school. One block of flats on that estate, on the Sutton Court Road side, close to Grove Park Bridge, was named "Montgomery Court" in honour of the Field Marshall who had been granted the Freedom of the Borough.

Sir Oswald Stoll's Chiswick Empire Theatre had continued to entertain the public throughout the many years since it was built, mainly with variety shows and pantomimes, although for a short period in the 1930's as a cinema, and the programme of variety items during the week commencing Monday 27th March 1959 was headed by a young man named Cliff Richards, supported by another artist by the name of Des O'Connor, both extremely well known today. Unfortunately, the Chiswick Empire closed later that year and was demolished, followed by the building of a parade of shops with a central tower block of offices named "Empire House" which was opened in 1961.

The old established and well known family butcher, whose premises adjoined that new development, "Caughts" also closed in 1960, and the site became part of another redevelopment, this time for John Lewis's "Waitrose" store.

Early winter in Chiswick House Grounds

Chiswick House on Christmas Day 1987

Strand-on-the-Green in the 1990's

Classic Bridge in Chiswick House

Further changes occurred in Chiswick during 1962, such as the withdrawal of the trolley buses, which were replaced by the very popular "Routemaster" motorbuses. Also, Christ Church Vicarage, which had been situated on the corner of Sutton Lane and Heathfield Gardens, opposite to Fromow's Corner, since it was built during the nineteenth century, was acquired for a new fire station, the Vicarage having first been replaced with a new house close by at number 2 Wellesley Road, complete with a garage. Following the demolition of the old Vicarage and clearance of the site, the new Fire Station was built in 1963, complete with a practice tower, and the new position of the station afforded easier access to the surrounding neighbourhood, a great improvement on the position of the old fire station which had been on the corner of the High Road and Linden Gardens, from where the engines frequently found themselves in the midst of congested traffic.

That site of the old fire station was subsequently used for the erection of a modern Police Station which had occupied somewhat restricted premises on the other side of the High Road, on the corner of Windmill Road, those old premises being retained for the use of probation officers.

"Thorncroft", an early eighteenth century house situated next to The Pack Horse & Talbot public house, and numbered 147 Chiswick High Road, had been the home for many years of Dr. Gilbert French, was demolished in 1965. Its rear garden was of great length extending behind the Chiswick Baptist Church in Annandale Road, and subsequently the garden land was incorporated into a Local Authority new housing development on the east side of Annandale Road.

Also in 1965, the map of England and Wales was redrawn whereby the old County boundaries, in many cases, were altered and new names appeared, sometimes in place of ancient and familiar names. One such, affecting Chiswick, was the ancient

County of Middlesex which was stripped of its administration and was replaced by an enlarged London County Council, renamed the Greater London Council, with individual Boroughs being amalgamated to form larger London Boroughs on an assumption that an authority of a larger area would prove more economical.

As a result of that process, as from 1st April 1965, the Borough of Brentford and Chiswick became part of the awkwardly shaped London Borough of Hounslow, having apparently been tacked onto the former Borough of Heston & Isleworth, as the western end of the new Borough.

When the Post Office services commenced in the middle of the nineteenth century, it was soon realised that there would be a need for sorting offices to be established to which mail could be dispatched for sorting and delivery to the addresses in the nearby area, and such a sorting office for the Chiswick local area was established before the end of the century, on the corner of Clifton Gardens with Back Common Lane, and when London was divided into postal districts, that sorting office became one of the West London areas, which apart from the central W1 and W2 areas were numbered alphabetically commencing with Acton (W3), then Chiswick (W4), Ealing (W5), Hammersmith (W6), Hanwell (W7), Kensington (W8), and so on to West Kensington (W14). However, that Clifton Gardens sorting office was closed during 1967, as also was the small Chiswick Main Post Office at numbers 257–259 Chiswick High Road, when a newly built combined Sorting and Post Office premises were opened in Prospect Place at the junction of Heathfield Terrace with Barley Mow Passage, between Devonshire Works (the former Sanderson Wallpaper factory) and the Army & Navy Depository.

Another event that had commenced in the middle of the nineteenth century, was the creation by the then Duke of Devonshire of an avenue of lime trees that swept southwards from Chiswick High Road into Chiswick House Grounds, which avenue was appropriately named "Dukes Avenue". A lodge house was built at the northern end of the avenue, on the corner of Bourne Place, named the "North Lodge" in 1851, but subsequently it ceased being a lodge and during the inter-war years it had become a conveniently placed depot for the United Dairies. However, during 1968, that depot closed and the North Lodge was demolished, the site eventually being acquired by the Roman Catholic Church and redeveloped as a Parish Centre.

One reason for the closure of the old Post Office Sorting Office in Clifton Gardens, was that all the houses in both that road and Holly Road as well as the surrounding area including Belmont Road and Grove, had been declared an area for redevelopment by the local authorities, and in due course demolition took place of most of the properties within the area which extended to include the east side of Fishers Lane, which had previously been occupied by sundry old sheds and stables which were used to house the stalls of local street barrow vendors. A road was created behind the shops in that part of the High Road, linked to an existing stretch of road, so that Belmont Road became linked with Fishers Lane, and one of the main buildings which was erected fronting that link road, was the Chiswick Health Centre. That linking road was given the name of Dolman Road, off which another new road was constructed running north, named Kirton Close a residential development which includes "Jessop House" a specially designed residential development for the elderly. Other housing, some of it very suitable for occupation by elderly people, was provided on the east side of Fishers Lane, and in another new road turning out of Fishers Lane, named Arnott Close.

About that same time, private developers decided that if it was possible to acquire a number of the large Victorian houses on the western side of Hartington Road, each with their long rear gardens reaching down to the river, it would be possible to carry out an attractive riverside development. Their first acquisition was such a house, number eleven, the elderly owner of which had died and his widow decided to move away. That house they had named "Rivercourt" as they were Methodists who attended their Chiswick Church, which in pre-war days was one of a number of churches in the Methodist Circuit known as the "Rivercourt Circuit" so named because the principal church in the Circuit was the Rivercourt Church on the corner of King Street and Rivercourt Road in Hammersmith. Thereafter a number of houses on each side of "Rivercourt" were purchased by agreement from the occupying vendors, and demolition afforded the developers the large, riverside site on which they built houses in various styles, carefully retaining commercial mooring rights, and the development was named "Chiswick Staithe".

A few years later, during 1971, Cubitts Yacht Basin was acquired by another developing company who decided to carry out works which enabled them to retain a marina type basin for use by the residents of the estate and to build modern style houses on the reclaimed land around the basin, and the development was given the name of "Chiswick Quay".

The British parliamentary boundaries were amended during 1971, resulting in Chiswick being placed within the constituency of Hounslow, Brentford & Isleworth, thereby losing its name in the title.

The new Chiswick Police Station was opened in 1971, on the corner of the High Road and Linden Gardens, the old police station situated on the opposite side of the High Road, being retained for probation officers. Also work commenced, in April of that year, on protecting properties along the river fronts against possible flooding, it having been realised that there existed considerable risk of serious damage by the higher tides being experienced along those tidal reaches of the River Thames. The protective work carried out to all the properties along Chiswick Mall and Strand-on-the-Green, some of which are extremely valuable, sometimes included the use of supported, toughened glass where the occupiers view of the river would otherwise have been obstructed.

Also, during 1971, considerable local opposition arose to the proposed action of the Chiswick Parochial Charities Trustees which would have involved the selling off of the Hopkin Morris Homes of Rest on Strand-on-the-Green, opposite to Magnolia Road. That opposition was led by the Old Folk's Fund whose honourary secretary was Mrs. Connie MacIntyre, J.P., also the Strand-on-the-Green Residents Association, and the matter was reported upon, at some length, in the Brentford & Chiswick Times between May and October of that year. On the flank of the Homes, fronting Strand-on-the-Green, is a plaque recording that the building of four alms houses was by Thomas Child, Soloman Williams and William Abbott (carpenter at his own charge) . . . "for ye use of poor of Chiswick for ever" and the date was altered from "1704" to "1724".

Alms houses existed on the site at least one hundred years before that date, and the Chiswick Parochial Charities Trustees were appointed to administer them in 1893. Before and after the First World War of 1914 to 1918, the Chiswick Parochial Charities Trustees had considered selling the Strand-on-the-Green alms houses in order to acquire a larger site in Burlington Lane from His Grace, the Duke of Devonshire, but Mr. Hopkin Morris opposed the sale and offered to pay for the conversion of the six existing alms houses into three good alms houses, and that conversion was completed in 1930, when the building was named the "Hopkin Morris Homes of Rest".

The oppositions raised in 1971 led the Chiswick Parochial Charities Trustees to agree to sell the Homes to the London Borough of Hounslow so that the proceeds could be used towards the building of Charity Homes in Edensor Road, named "Whittington Court". The Local Council then set in motion a scheme to renovate the Homes under the direction of their architect, Mr. G.A. Trevett, which resulted in Messrs. Green, Lloyd & Adams, architects, being commissioned to carry out the agreed works.

These works were eventually completed in 1975, and was of sufficient interest to be brought to the attention of the R.I.C.S.-Times Conservation Awards Committee resulting in the scheme being considered worthy of a Commendation, and during September of 1976, a ceremony took place at the Hounslow Civic Centre, when the Commendation Certificate was handed over by Mr. V.D. Revell, the Chairman of the Middlesex & Urban Essex Branch of the Royal Institution of Chartered Surveyors, to Mr. B.L. Adams, the architect, and the Chairman of the Hounslow Housing Committee, Councillor the Rev. Baden Pearce, at which ceremony the author was present. Report of the ceremony can be found in the Brentford & Chiswick Times of 30th September 1976.

Whilst those events were occurring, one of Chiswick's most prominent National Schools, on the corner of Heathfield Terrace and Horticultural Place, facing Turnham Green, was demolished in 1972. From the time it had ceased to be used as a school, the building had been used by the Local Authority as offices for Sanitary Inspectors, now more politely referred to as "Environment Health Officers".

In the same year that Great Britain became a member of the European Economic Council, 1973, Christ Church on Turnham Green, celebrated its one hundred and fiftieth anniversary. The Parish of Christ Church, Turham Green, had been created in 1841 to accommodate the increasing population, the only other Anglican Church in the Chiswick area being St. Nicholas by the river in Old Chiswick.

Sir Gilbert Scott, R.A. was commissioned to design an appropriate church to be built on land at Turnham Green granted by the Dean & Chapter of St. Paul's Cathedral, as the Lord of the Manor of Little Sutton, and when the building was completed it was consecrated by the Bishop of London on 27th April 1843. During 1887, the year in which Queen Victoria celebrated her golden jubilee, some extensions were added to Christ Church.

Another anniversary occurred in 1973 when the well known firm of surveyors, valuers, auctioneers and estate agents, Messrs. Tyser, Greenwood & Company celebrated the centenary of the firm's establishment in 1873, by Mr. Richard Tyser, and shortly after that celebration the two senior partners, Mr. H. Norman Harding, F.R.I.C.S., F.A.I. and Mr. Ernest J. Griffen, F.A.I., retired leaving the business in the hands of the two junior partners, Mr. George S. Bradley, F.A.I. and Mr. William P. Roe, F.R.I.C.S., F.A.I.

It was about that time that development, or redevelopment, of sites within the Chiswick area became more evident, such as the proposal to develop a site between Milnthorpe and Park Roads which involved the unforeseen felling of a number of trees, which led to very strong opposition from members of the Chiswick House Residents Association. Some building of houses was finally permitted by the local Planning Authority, but it was confined to a reasonable number of houses only, and in a back-handed acknowledgement of that opposition, the developers named the new houses "CHARA PLACE"

Another area of redevelopment was the old railway sidings used primarily for coal supplies, which gradually fell into disuse after the coming into effect of the Clean Air Act of 1956. That site was on the north side of Chiswick High Road, beyond Cleveland Avenue, and it was used to build an estate of houses given the name of "Ravensmede Way".

The West London Timber Works had occupied a site between the railway line which passed across the southern end of Whitehall Park Road and the eastern ends of Herbert and Ernest Gardens, off Magnolia Road, in the Strand-on-the-Green area, where a small estate of houses was built.

St. Joseph's Home in Burlington Lane, a haven for elderly and infirm ladies, cared for by the sisterhood known as the Society of St. Margaret, had decided to change its name to St. Mary's Convent, and there evolved a desire to provide more and improved accommodation for their ladies. One means of raising funds for that project was to sell off some of their extensive garden land now that the demand for development sites had enhanced the likely selling price. That led to some of the land on the perimeter of their grounds being sold for residential development, that on the Corney Road frontage being named "Dartmouth Place", whilst that on the Burlington Lane frontage, an area backing onto Powell's Walk, was used for the erection of other houses named "Langham Place".

The London Borough of Hounslow published, in 1984, their "Chiswick Local Plan" which indicated proposed redevelopment changes, some of which were already in the process and other expected to take place, although not all materialised.

The old Star & Garter Hotel, at the foot of Kew Bridge on the corner of Spring Grove, ceased to exist as such and was converted into offices.

The site of the old Brentford Fruit and Vegetable Market, just west of the Great West Road in the High Road, was subsequently redeveloped, partly for industrial units, but mainly as a local authority pleasure unit, including a swimming pool, named after the fountain which, at one time, occupied the nearby site at the foot of Kew Bridge.

Elsewhere in the business section of Chiswick, there occurred the proposed redevelopment of the site of what had been Whitbreads bottling plant, which occupied a large area north of the High Road and east of Acton Lane, with the main entrance through Essex Place Square from Chiswick High Road. It adjoined the site of Pope's Depository premises in Acton Lane, and Fromow's Market Garden land just south of the railway line beside Chiswick Park Railway Station, on which site there had been a proposal to redevelop as high rise office accommodation.

However, the age of supermarkets resulted in Sainsbury's becoming interested in acquiring all three areas for their redevelopment as one of their supermarkets with ample car parking facilities.

An area of land rear of the Chiswick Town Hall and the adjoining terrace of period properties, which had been beautifully renovated by the Hazelmere Group following the cessation of their use by the local authority, was developed to provide offices for the Social Services and other private purposes, off Horticultural Place. The original plan to provide new public library premises on that site had, unfortunately, not met with the full approval of the local residents.

A site in the residential area of Chiswick between Sutton Lane, Burnaby Gardens and Harvard Hill, which had previously been occupied for many years as the Gunnersbury Preparatory School, was acquired and redeveloped residentially. Yet another site that was made available for residential redevelopment, was an area of land north of Thames Road and east of Strand-on-the-Green School, beside the Southern railway line between Kew Bridge Station and Chiswick Station. Part of that site had been occupied for many years by the Parks Packing Company alongside a small recreation ground behind the cottages in Thames Road that had been demolished by enemy action in the form of a "land-mine" in 1940. That redevelopment now has the name "Oliver Close", so named after the island in the River Thames off Strand-on-the-Green, to which, it is claimed, Oliver Cromwell fled when threatened by Royalist troops after the Battle of Brentford.

Mention has been made earlier of the local authority's development of an area north of the Chiswick High Road which included the erection of the Chiswick Health Centre plus residential accommodation to the west of Fisher's Lane. Now an area on the east side of Fisher's Lane, which had been occupied by the Primitive Methodist Chapel until it was bombed during the second world war, also other premises in Chiswick Common Road which had been variously occupied, including a transport depot, was acquired and redeveloped as homes for elderly people and was named "Homecross House".

The old Tram Depot and its power house, on the north side of the High Road, to the west of Merton Avenue, had become a bus depot, but the adjoining power house had ceased to be required with the abolition of trolley buses. The requirement of more residential accommodation resulted in the upper section of the power house being converted into residential units and suitably named the "Power House" the lower section being converted into a recording studio.

In the meantime the Old Bus Depot in Belmont Road, from which the open topped buses were sent over to France during the first world war to transport troops, had been abandoned and remained unoccupied for some years, although many local residents thought that the premises could usefully be occupied by a multi-storey car park. Pleads to that effect were ignored, however, and in due course the site was acquired for more residential housing and given the name of "Alfred Close".

During the second world war the Times Furnishing Company's premises on the corner of Chiswick High Road and Dukes Avenue, was bombed and it remained as a bombed site for many years thereafter due, it was widely believed, because the planning authority refused to allow the rebuilding to occupy the entire site of the previous premises. Eventually the Times Furnishing Company did develop a shop on that part of the site permitted, but it failed to attract the trade previously experienced, partly due to the gradual decline of the Chiswick High Road shopping area, many of the shops having changed from trading to service facilities such as betting shops; building societies; restaurants; cafes and estate agents.

More recently the Times Furnishing Company's site was acquired for a Barratt's redevelopment, a complex of shops on the ground floor with residential flats above which were given the name of "Chatsworth Lodge". Before that, however, the well known developers had acquired the site of the former Central School on the south side of Staveley Road, which had closed not long after it had become part of the new Chiswick Comprehensive School arrangement, and which became surplus to requirements when there were fewer pupils requiring places in the local Comprehensive School, which continued at the nearby former Grammar School in Burlington Lane.

The site of the Central School including playing fields which extended back from Staveley Road with a long return frontage in Burlington Lane, and as one of the entrances into Chiswick House Grounds is in Staveley Road, immediately opposite to the demolished Central Secondary Education School, the plan to develop the site was inspired by the lay out of the grounds of Chiswick House, a fact which won the development much praise and an award. The estate was named "Chiswick Place" and the roads within the development were given the names of Fitzroy Crescent; Crofton Avenue and Huntingdon Gardens.

The year of 1987 will probably be remembered by many people for three events, firstly the General Election in June which again returned a government led by Margaret Thatcher; secondly, for the appalling terrorist bombing at the Enniskillen Remembrance Service in Northern Ireland; and locally for the hurricane force winds experienced during one night in October, causing havoc with fallen and falling trees in virtually every street and forcing the temporary closure of both the Royal Botanic Gardens at Kew and Chiswick House Grounds.

That was followed during the next year by more winds of

change when the Greater London Council was abolished and the individual London Boroughs authorised to run their own affairs.

The Trustees of the Chiswick Methodist Church had for some years been aware of the need to reorganise the quite extensive premises which they occupied between the Great West Road Extension and Barrowgate Road, particularly when the Manse, number 25 Sutton Court Road, became surplus to requirement for the housing of a Church Minister. The increase in the value of sites for residential redevelopment made it possible for sufficient funds to be available upon the sale of some of the land following the demolition of the large church sited on the corner of Barrowgate Road, and the old School Hall which had been built in 1880, as well as the Manse, and to use the site of the Manse and part of the site of the School Hall, for the erection of a smaller, dual-purpose Church and Hall, the remaining site, fronting Barrowgate Road being sold off and redeveloped with some fine houses.

Way back in 1871, a large Depot for the storage of furniture, etc. was built alongside premises which had been military barracks and a drill hall at the Prospect Place end of both Heathfield Terrace and Barley Mow Passage, and that depot became known as the Army and Navy Depot. The building was impressive and very solidly constructed so approval was given for the premises to be converted principally for residential units although some business units were also made available to one section. The new redeveloped premises was given the name of "Devonhurst Place".

The old Chiswick Open Air Swimming Baths had been closed and left to further deteriorate but the need for more residential accommodation caused the local authority to give consideration to the persistent local demand that the Baths be reinstated. Plans were approved for more development in Edensor Road extending eastward towards Pumping Station Road, and extending down towards the river. Blocks of flats named Edensor Gardens were already built and occupied and on Edensor Road a small, partly commercial unit named Dolphin Square, was created with the New Chiswick Swimming Bath accommodated between it and Edensor Gardens. Also, two other residential developments took place beside and to the south of Edensor Gardens, named Claremont Grove and Anstice Close.

Whilst that development was proceeding, work had been carried out to the office tower block adjacent to Gunnersbury Railway Station, which for many years had been occupied by the International Business Machines Company, and during 1994 the block was taken over by the British Standards Institute.

St. Mary's Convent and Nursing Home has been mentioned previously, and in 1996 celebrations occurred to mark the centenary of its foundation in Chiswick. Her Royal Highness, the Princess Alexandra, had become Patron for the Centenary Year and a series of events took place throughout the year. The work of the Sisterhood, who have homes throughout the world, is to provide a peaceful haven for the elderly and infirm with very careful medical nursing care. Although periphery land had been sold off, there still remains an extensive, beautifully kept, garden for the enjoyment of the residents and visitors.

Right against the border with Hammersmith, another residential redevelopment took place in British Grove (so named after one of the earliest British National Schools which existed there), the redevelopment comprising the building of a terrace of three storey, mews-type houses.

One of the more extensive redevelopments however was gradually taking place, after years of careful planning and consultation, involving an area of riverside land which had been used for many years to accommodate local authority depots and for other commercial purposes. The stretch of the River Thames between Chiswick Eyot and Dukes Meadows has been known at least since the seventeenth century, as Corney Reach, so named after Corney

House which had been built on that river frontage, just south of St. Nicholas Church, by Sir William Russell whose son became the 4th Earl of Bedford. During the early part of the nineteenth century, Corney House was acquired by the Duke of Devonshire and the old house was demolished. Never-the-less, the name of Corney Road was given to the road from Burlington Lane, beside St. Mary's Convent, joining a road which runs parallel to the river which was named Pumping Station Road.

The new development was on land between that road and the river, and between Edensor Road and Edensor Gardens, and the already fairly new residential development at Church Wharf, south-east of St. Nicholas Church, at the North-eastern end of the extended Pumping Station Road.

Great care was taken in the preparation for that new development, provision being made for a riverside walkway along its entire length, also for the creation of a Boating Pier onto the waterfront of the River Thames.

Some fine residential buildings were built, contained in fairly confined sections, and were given names most of which reflected connections with past usage of the immediate area, including Thames Crescent; Corney Reach Way; Malthouse Drive; Oast Lodge; Malting Lodge; Osier Mews; Russell Close; Lattimer Place, and in Pumping Station Road, Monet House; Chesterman Court; Nicholas Court and Willow Court. One section of the area has still to be developed as this is being written.

For some seventy years there existed a motor showroom, garage with petrol supply pumps, on the corner of Sutton Court Road and Lawford Road, close to the foot of the Grove Park Bridge over the railway, but that garage closed in 1997 and the buildings demolished to make way for a row of houses which were given the name of "The Lawfords", due to be completed during 1998.

A small area of undeveloped land at the eastern end of Herbert Gardens, off Magnolia Road, in the Strand-on-the-Green area of

Chiswick, was acquired by builders who commenced building thirteen Mews style houses which they named "Chiswick Gate".

Also in the meantime, a comparatively small site on the south side of Chesterfield Road, close to its junction with Chatsworth Road, was redeveloped with a pair of houses sympathetically designed to blend with the existing adjoining houses of unusual front elevation, and those houses were expected to be completed during 1998, and were given the name of "Park Villas".

The London General Omnibus Company during the middle of the nineteenth century, began controlling the various existing omnibus routes in their area. Originally the omnibus consisted of a single-deck carriage with passengers seated facing each other, and the carriage was drawn by a pair of horses. Well before the end of that century, the omnibuses were provided with seats on their upper deck approached by an external staircase at the rear, but there was no covering to those seats on the upper deck. Then the internal combustion engine replaced the horses and at the beginning of the twentieth century an engineer works was established by the London General Omnibus Company, on the north side of Chiswick High Road, opposite to Gunnersbury Railway Station. Those works remained in active service for some eighty years before being closed down and the buildings demolished. Plans for a "business park" were approved and work commenced but ground to a halt and the site remained unused for some years, although during 1998, it was announced that an Anglo-Norwegian Group of international engineers were planning new head quarters on that site.

One of the Gothic houses at the Strand-on-the-Green end of Grove Park Road, which possessed extensive garden land reaching down to the river, had been adapted and extended as a non-conformist college of training for Christian missionaries, and was known as Radcliffe College. By the mid-1990's, however, the premises were vacated by the college and by 1998 much of the old buildings had been demolished and a commencement made on the erection of new residential accommodation, as yet unnamed.

During the past decade, or so, very many two floored, villa type houses in the Chiswick area, have utilised their extensive roof space and formed a third floor, normally with dormer style windows in the rear roof slope, and with roof slope skylights on the front elevation.

As the year 2000 is approached, one wonders what changes will take place in Chiswick, during the next century.